SELECTIONS FROM

ELEGIES
A SONG CYCLE
by WILLIAM FINN

T0055165

All piano arrangements by
Vadim Feichtner and Carmel Dean

Photo: Joan Marcus

WILLIAM FINN (Lyrics/Director) is currently represented on Broadway with The 25th Annual Putnam County Spelling Bee. Finn is the writer/composer of *Falsettos* (two Tony Awards: Best Book, with James Lapine, and Best Original Score). He has written/composed *In Trousers* (L.A. Drama Critics Award), *March of the Falsettos* (Outer Critics Circle Award for Outstanding Musical, L.A. Drama Critics Award), *Falsettoland* (two Drama Desk Awards and Lucille Lortel Award for Best Musical), *Romance in Hard Times* (Public Theater), *A New Brain* (Lincoln Center/ Outer Critics Circle Award for Best Musical) and *Elegies: A Song Cycle* (Lincoln Center). Finn wrote the lyrics to Graciela Daniele's *Tango Apasionado* (music by the great Astor Piazolla) and with Michael Starobin, the music to James Lapine's version of *The Winter's Tale*. With Vadim Feichtner he composed the music for the Public Theater's Central Park production of *As You Like*. For television, Mr. Finn provided the music and lyrics for the Ace Award-winning HBO cartoon "Ira Sleeps Over" and the score for "Poky Little Puppy's First Christmas." With Ellen Fitzhugh, he wrote the two next "Brave Little Toaster" cartoons. He graduated from Williams College, where he was awarded the Hutchinson Fellowship in Musical Composition, and currently teaches a weekly master class at NYU's Graduate Musical Theatre Writing Program.

Contents

MISTER CHOI AND MADAME G

Words and Music by
WILLIAM FINN

run, I think,_____ by East-ern Eu - ro-pe - ans

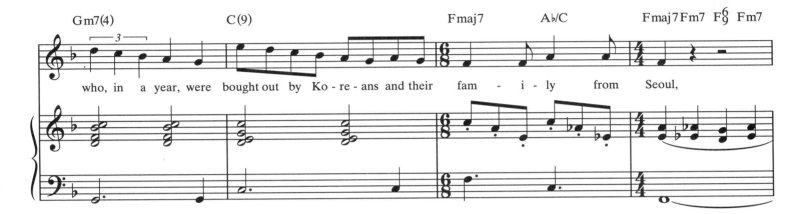

who, in a year, were bought out by Ko-re-ans and their fam - i - ly from Seoul,

who fed me at their fam-i-ly sink. We ate_____ kim - chi_____

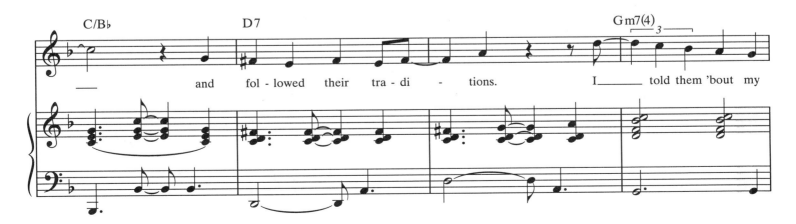

___ and fol - lowed their tra - di - tions. I_____ told them 'bout my

6

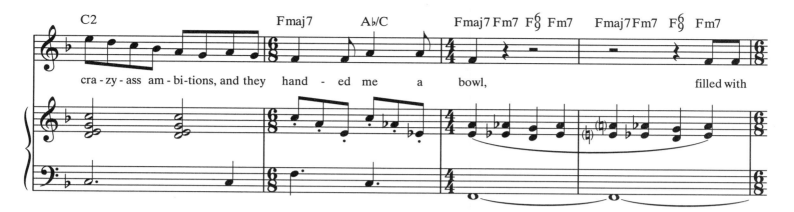

cra - zy - ass am - bi-tions, and they hand - ed me a bowl, filled with

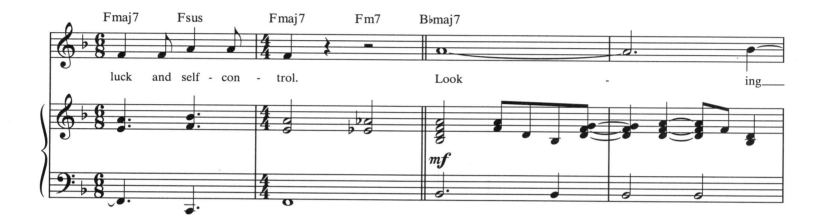

luck and self - con - trol. Look - ing

in the win - dow of this emp -

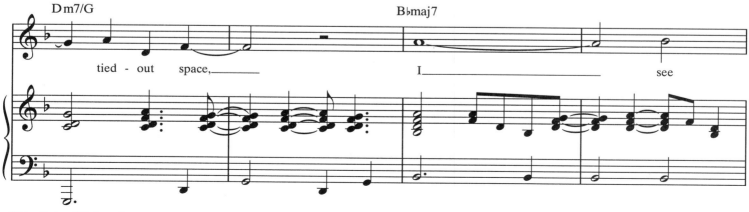

tied - out space, I see

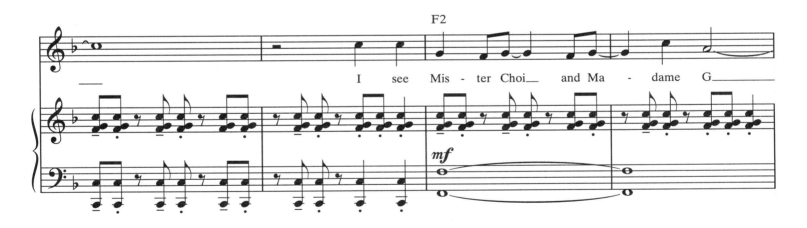

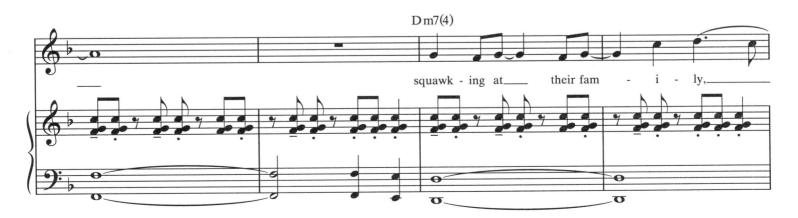

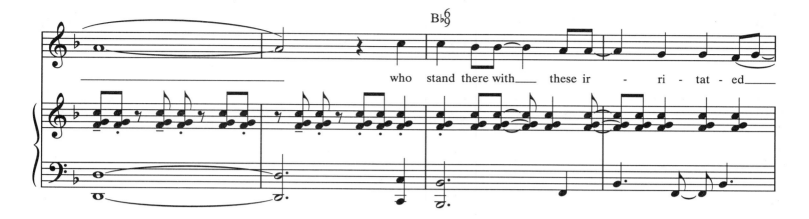

who stand there with ___ these ir - ri - tat - ed ___

___ grins. The chil - dren al - ways prac - tic - ing ___ their

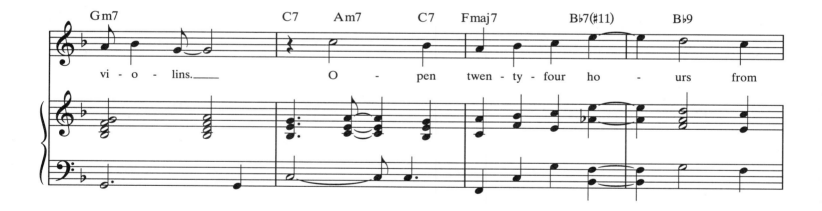

vi - o - lins. ___ O - pen twen - ty - four ho - urs from

dawn 'til ___ dawn. ___ And one day

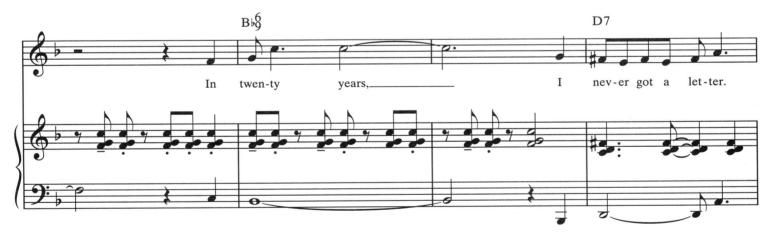

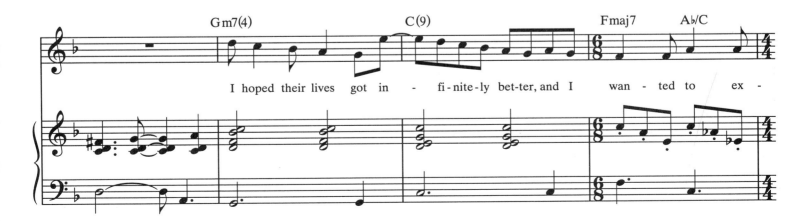

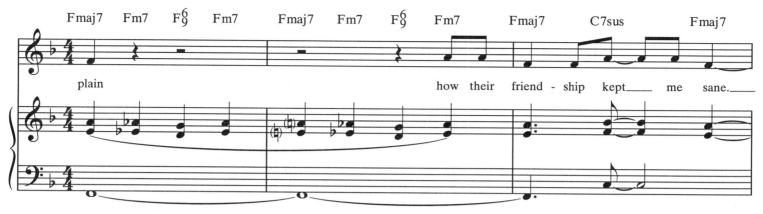

MARK'S ALL-MALE THANKSGIVING

Words and Music by
WILLIAM FINN

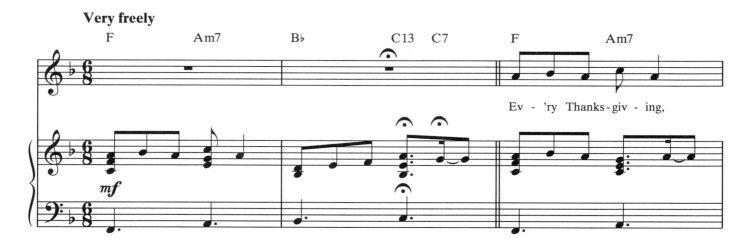

Ev - 'ry Thanks - giv - ing,

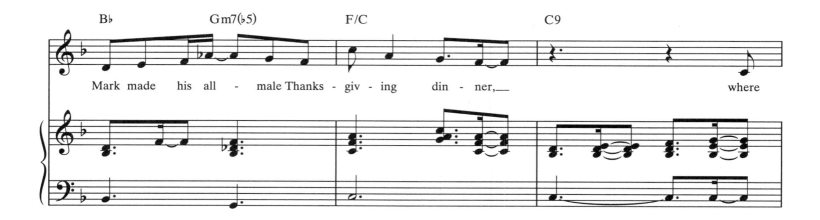

Mark made his all - male Thanks - giv - ing din - ner, ___ where

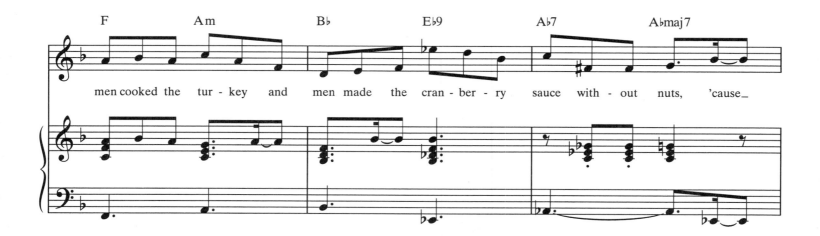

men cooked the tur - key and men made the cran - ber - ry sauce with - out nuts, 'cause ___

Mark's All-Male Thanksgiving - 8 - 1
25395

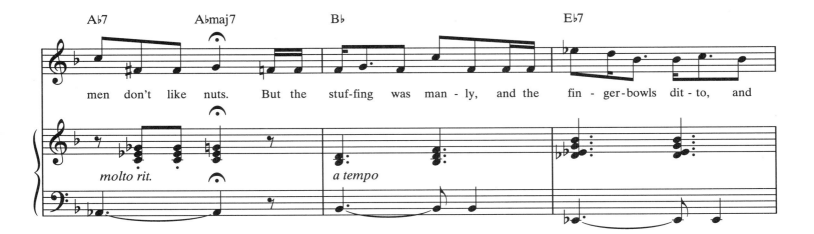

men don't like nuts. But the stuf-fing was man - ly, and the fin - ger-bowls dit - to, and

molto rit.

a tempo

dit - to the pu - reed sweet yams. Ver - y____ man - ly, when

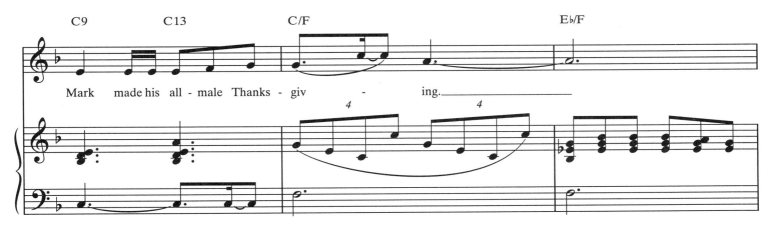

Mark made his all - male Thanks - giv - ing.____

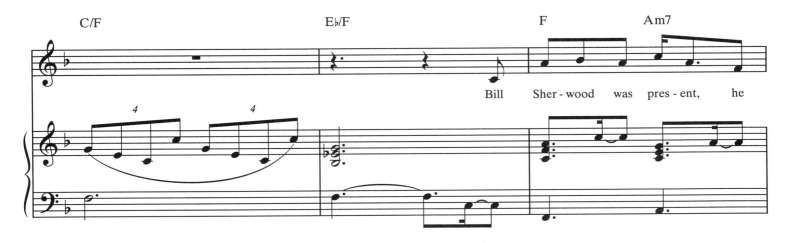

Bill Sher - wood was pres - ent, he

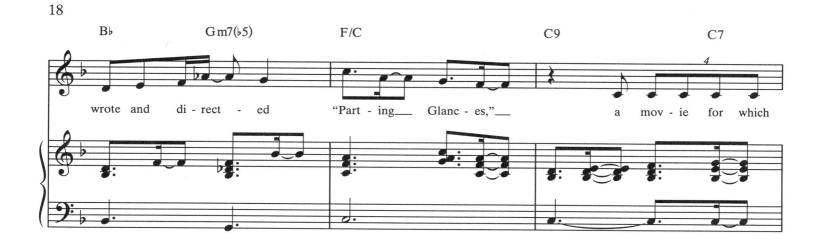

wrote and di-rect-ed "Part-ing___ Glanc-es,"___ a mov-ie for which

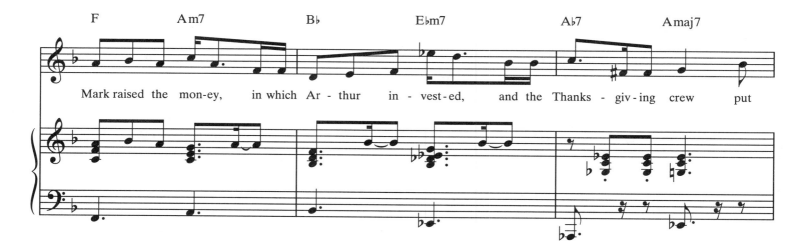

Mark raised the mon-ey, in which Ar-thur in-vest-ed, and the Thanks-giv-ing crew put

mon-ey in too. Steve Bus-ce-mi was fea-tured, his first time on screen, and you

knew you were watch-ing a star. God, he was great, but he

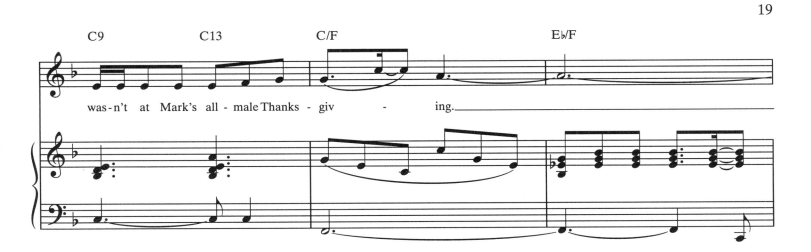

was-n't at Mark's all-male Thanks-giv - ing._____

Steady half-time feel

_____ Re-mem-ber-ing this_____ is sort of like

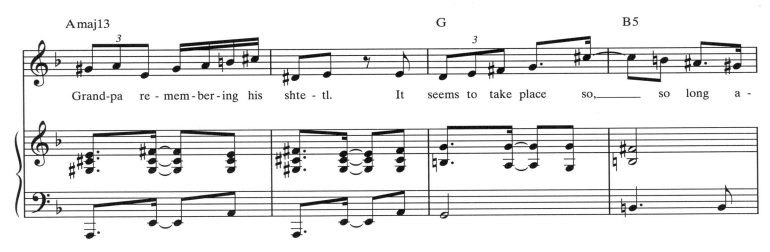

Grand-pa re-mem-ber-ing his shte-tl. It seems to take place so,_____ so long a-

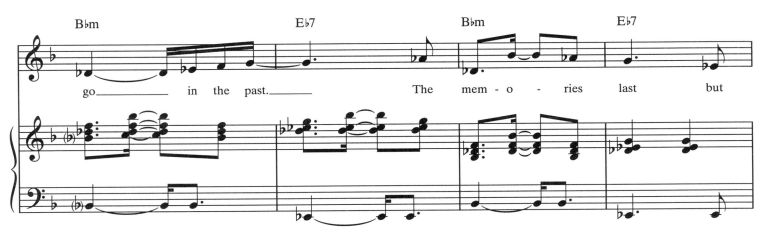

go_____ in the past._____ The mem-o-ries last but

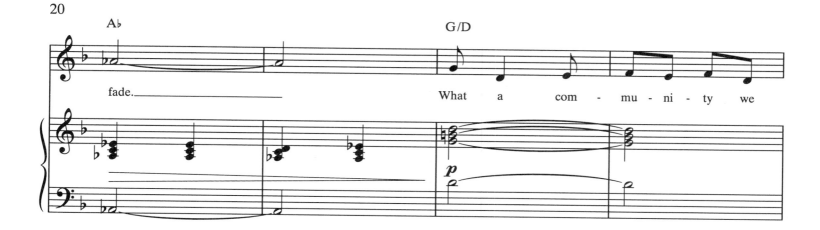

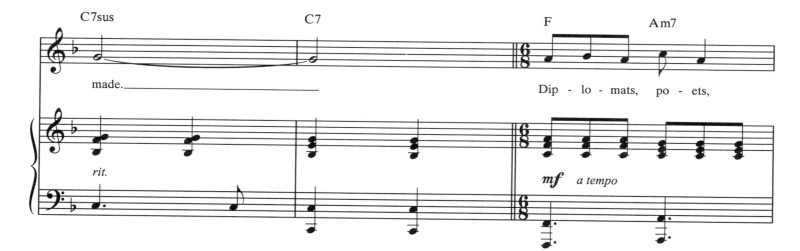

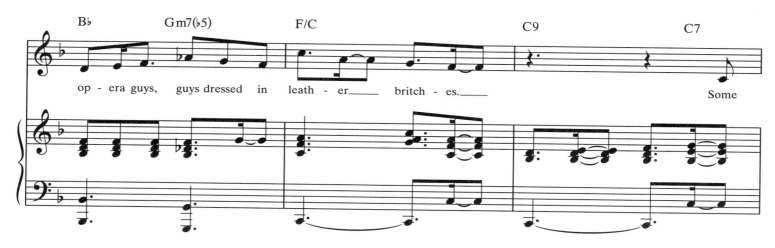

non - threat -'ning way. Mark, the law-yer, wore flan-nel, he comes from Wis - con - sin. The

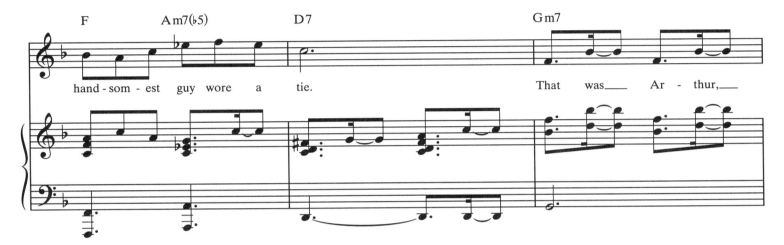

hand - som - est guy wore a tie. That was___ Ar - thur,___

sweet - ly de - cent, fun - ny and liv – ing._____

Freely

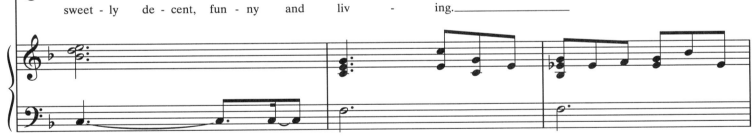

I met___ Ar - thur when Mark made his all - male Thanks - giv - ing.___

a tempo

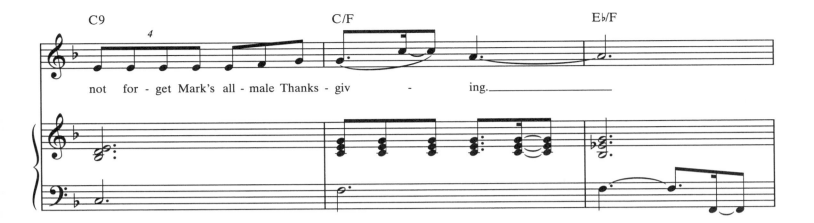

not for-get Mark's all-male Thanks-giv - ing._____

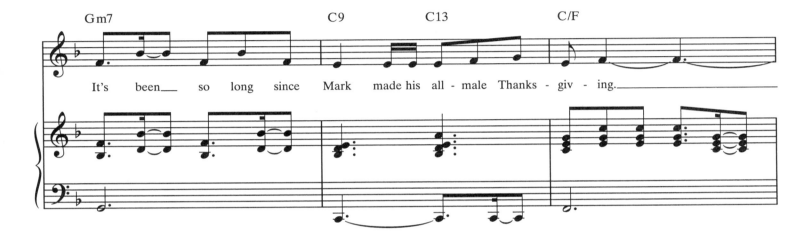

It's been___ so long since Mark made his all-male Thanks-giv - ing._____

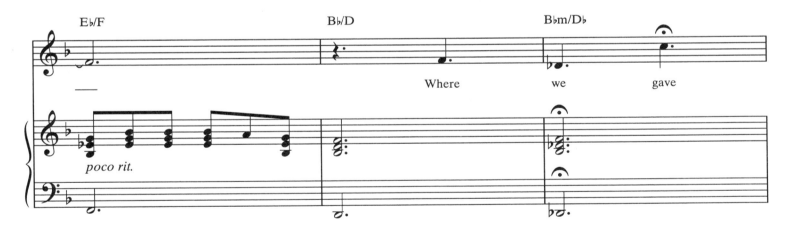

Where we gave

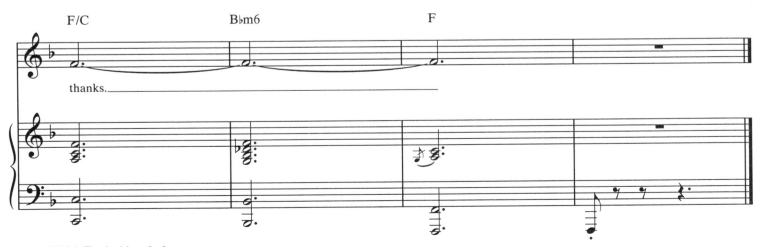

thanks._____

ONLY ONE

Words and Music by
WILLIAM FINN

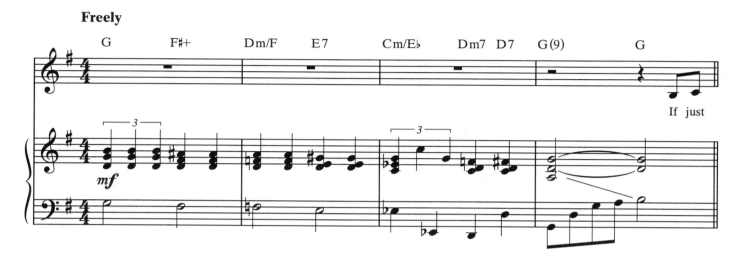

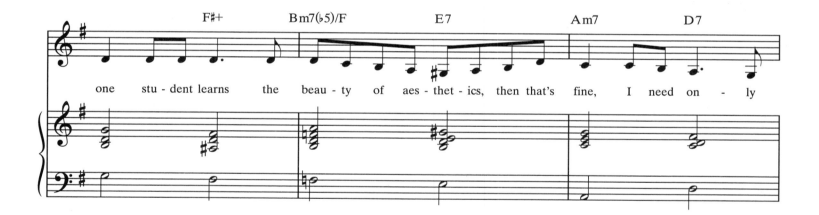

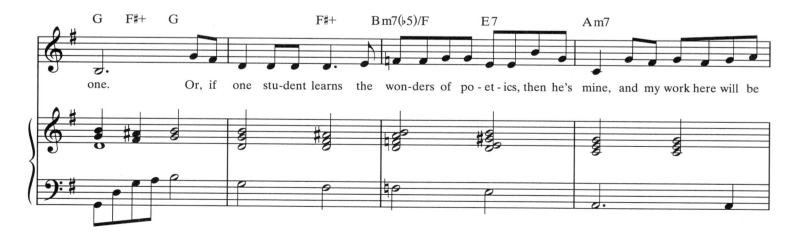

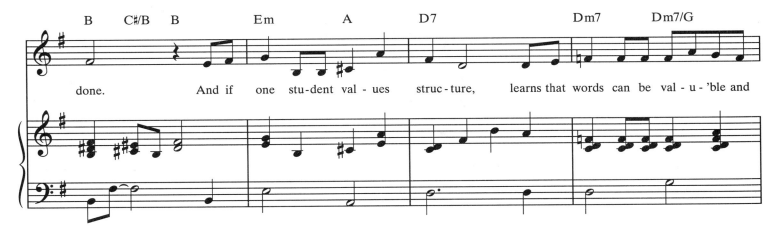

done. And if one stu-dent val-ues struc-ture, learns that words can be val-u-'ble and

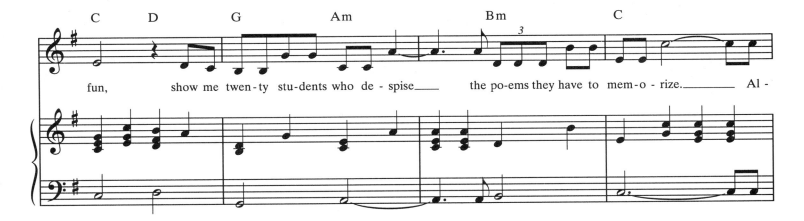

fun, show me twen-ty stu-dents who de-spise___ the po-ems they have to mem-o-rize.___ Al-

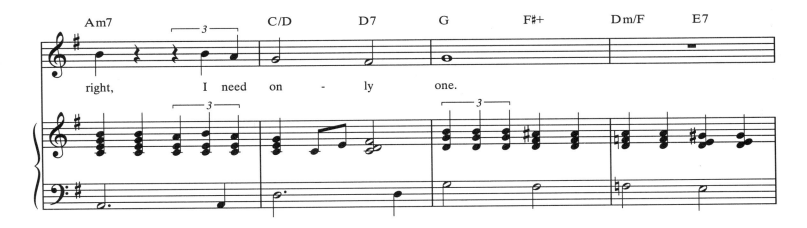

right, I need on - ly one.

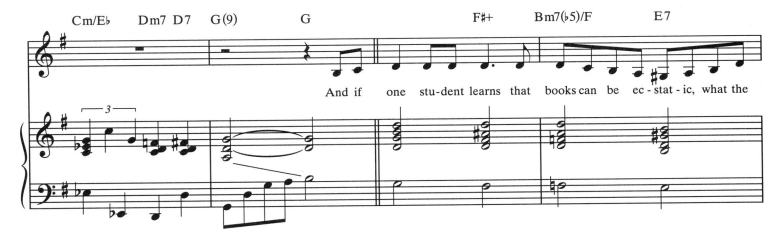

And if one stu-dent learns that books can be ec-stat-ic, what the

rare - ly watch - es tel - e - vi - sion. One stu - dent who

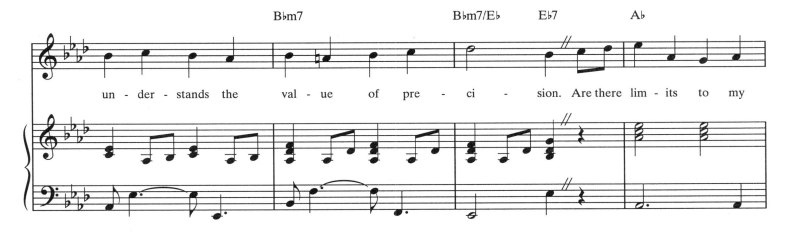

un - der - stands the val - ue of pre - ci - sion. Are there lim - its to my

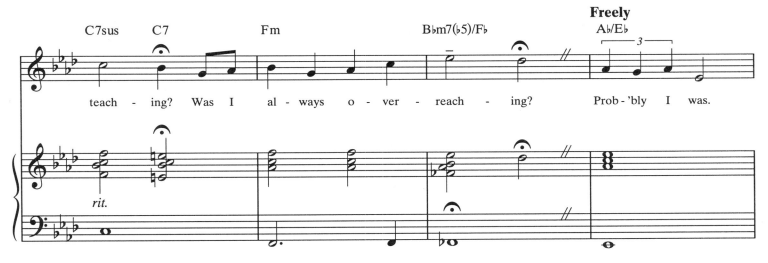

teach - ing? Was I al - ways o - ver - reach - ing? Prob - 'bly I was.

Freely

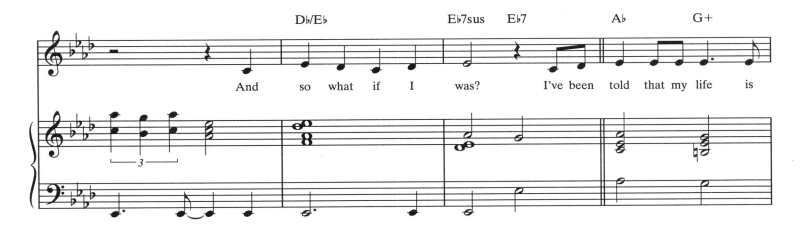

And so what if I was? I've been told that my life is

Grandly

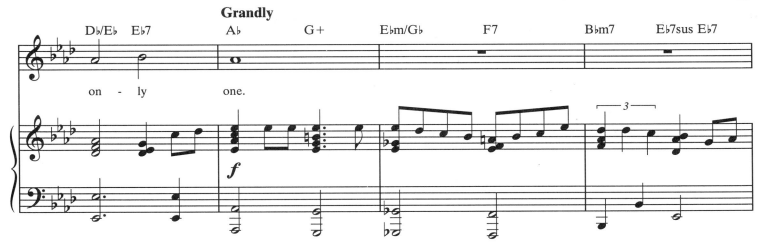

on - ly one.

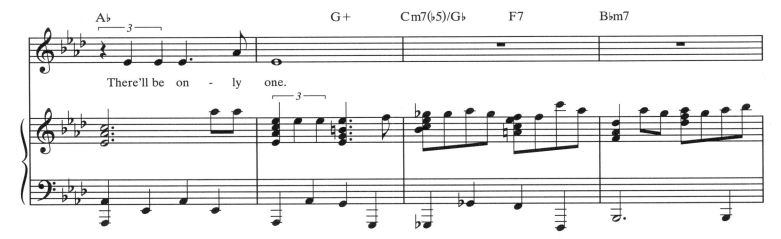

There'll be on - ly one.

There'll be on - ly one._____ There'll be on - ly one, on - ly

one. Da da da_____ da da da da da da_____

da da da da da   da da da da da.

So I'll live with the fact that I'm

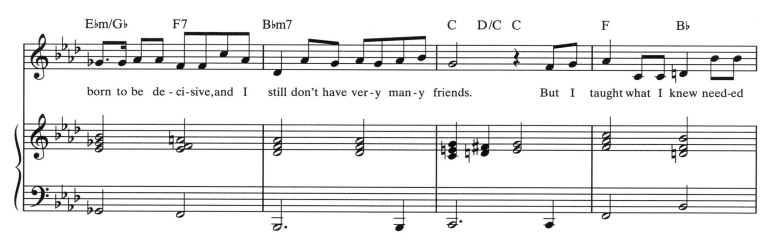

prick-ly and de-ri-sive, that I will, and not make a-mends. I was born with-out tact, I was

born to be de-ci-sive, and I still don't have ver-y man-y friends. But I taught what I knew need-ed

31

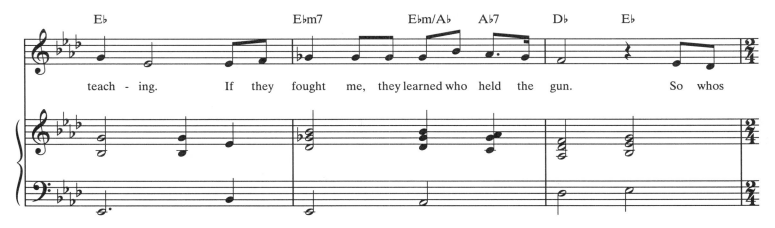

teach - ing. If they fought me, they learned who held the gun. So whos

stu - dents al - ways did the best_____ on ev - 'ry state - wide es - say test?

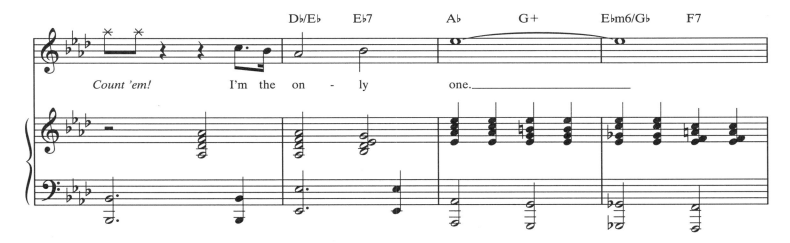

Count 'em! I'm the on - ly one._____

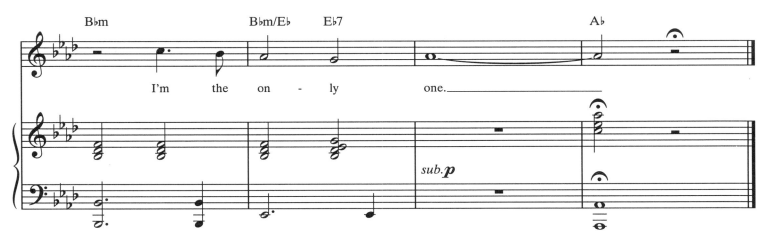

I'm the on - ly one._____

sub. ***p***

Only One - 8 - 8
25395

PASSOVER

Words and Music by
WILLIAM FINN

On this day____

we read__ of plagues_ and mis-for-tunes, then start eat - ing.____

Un-cle Har-vey's the cook. Ma laughs so loud that she shook. Cous - in Gar - y

is read - ing porn. We've run out of skull - caps. Some men are wear-ing

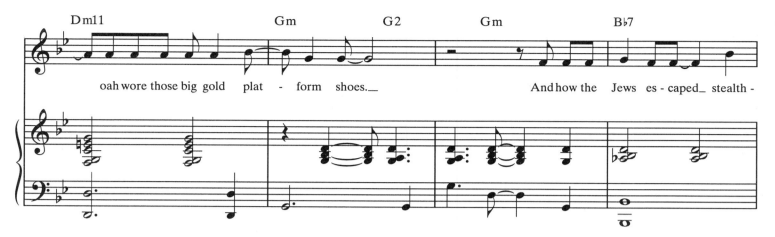

oah wore those big gold plat - form shoes.___ And how the Jews es - caped_ stealth -

ful - ly by split - ting the Red Sea.___

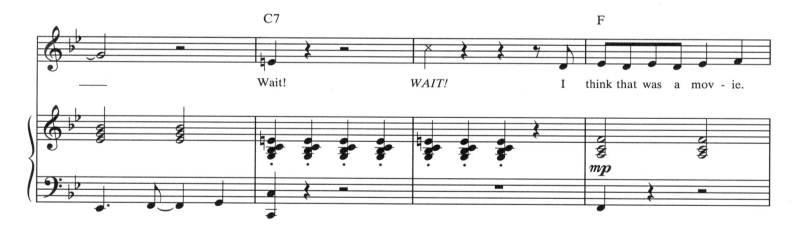

Wait! *WAIT!* I think that was a mov - ie.

An - y - way, when I tell the sto - ry of Pass - o - ver

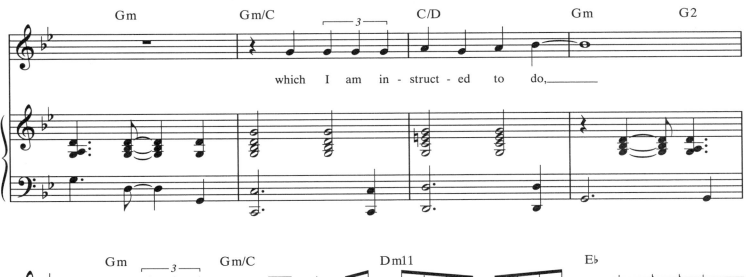

which I am in-struct-ed to do,_____

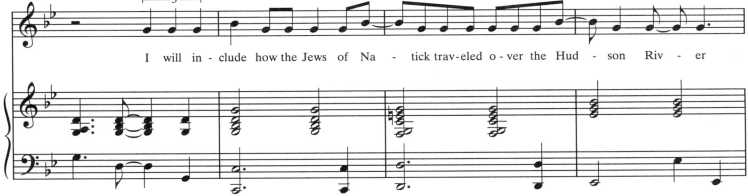

I will in-clude how the Jews of Na - tick trav-eled o - ver the Hud - son Riv - er

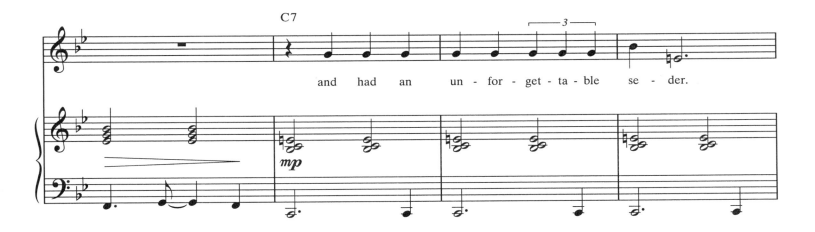

and had an un - for - get - ta - ble se - der.

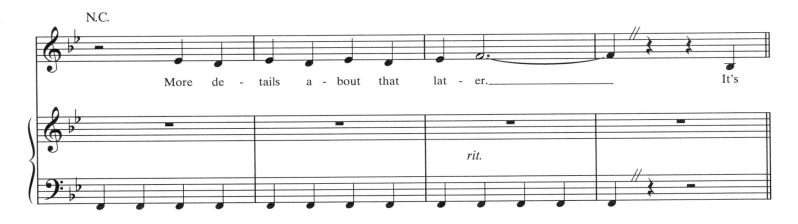

More de - tails a - bout that lat - er._____ It's

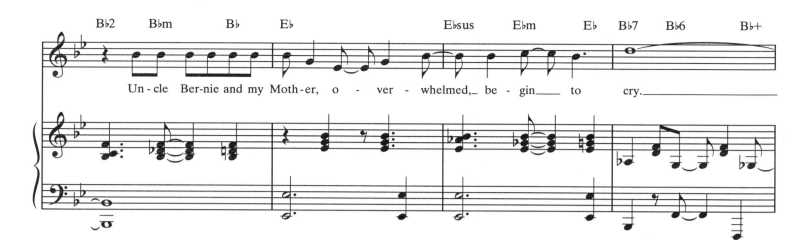

Un-cle Ber-nie and my Moth-er, o - ver - whelmed,_ be - gin__ to cry._____

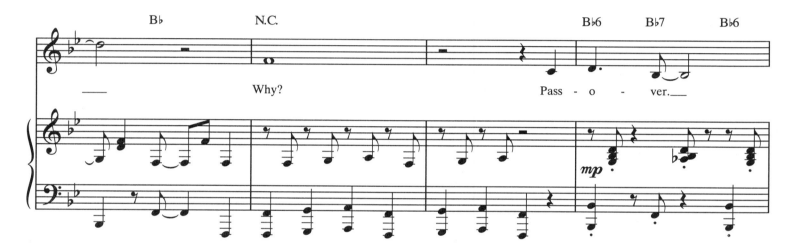

__ Why? Pass - o - ver.__

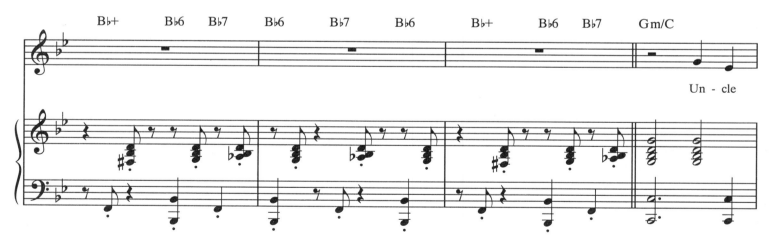

Un - cle

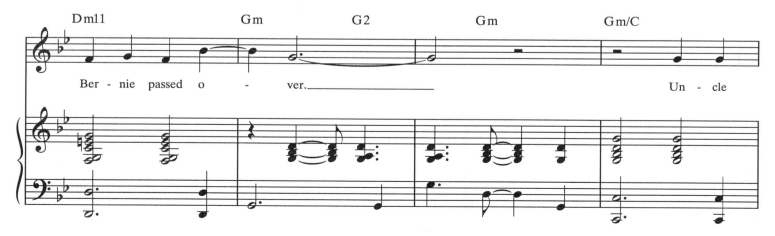

Ber - nie passed o - ver._____ Un - cle

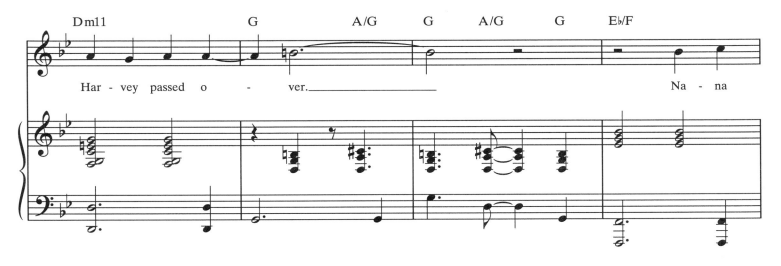

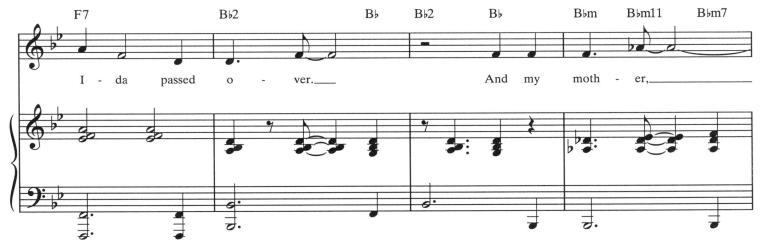

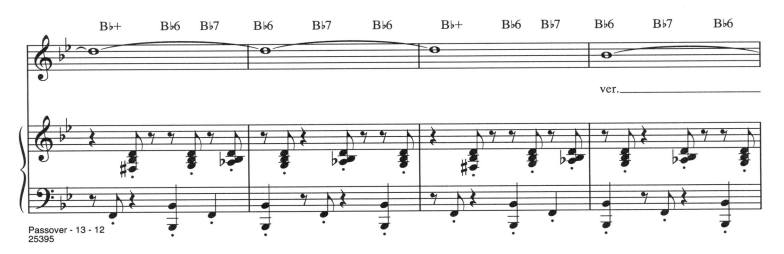

INFINITE JOY

Words and Music by
WILLIAM FINN

Moderately slow (♩ = 82)

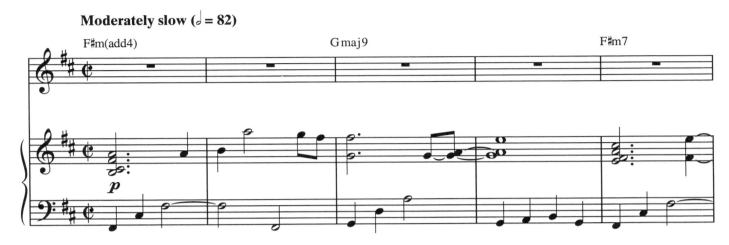

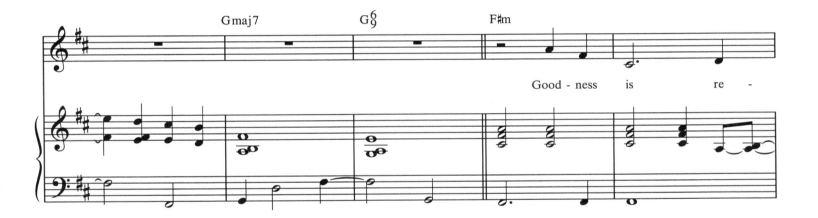

Good - ness is re -

ward - ed. Hope is guar - an - teed.____

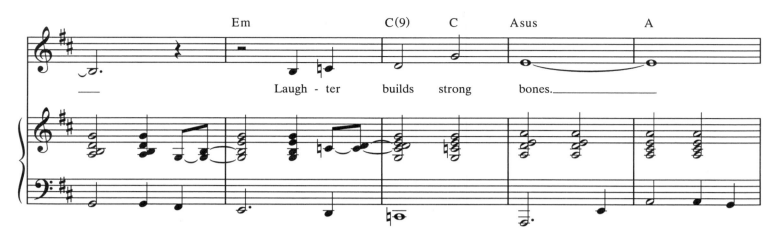

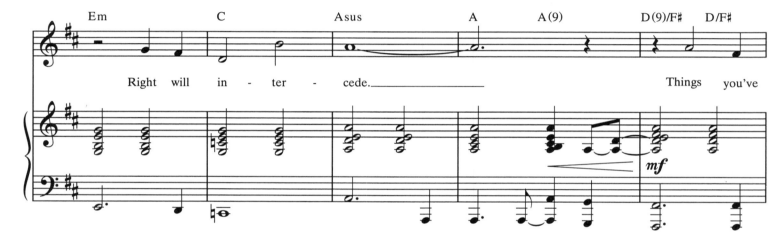

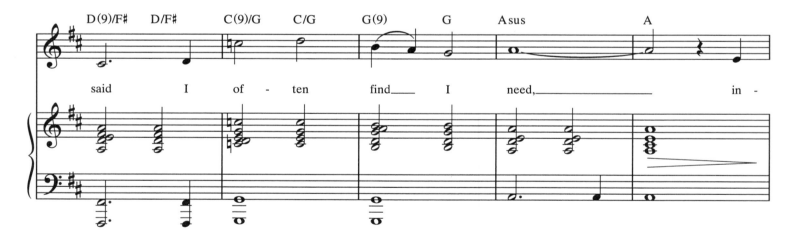

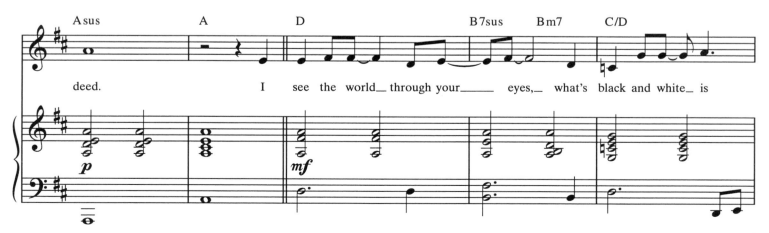

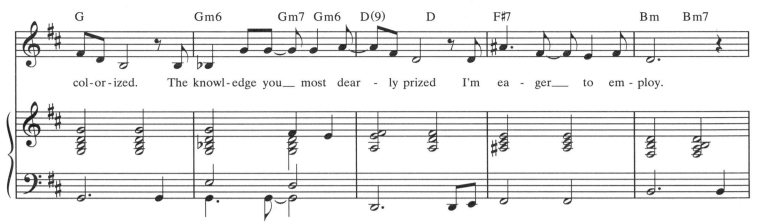

col-or-ized. The knowl-edge you__ most dear-ly prized I'm ea-ger__ to em-ploy.

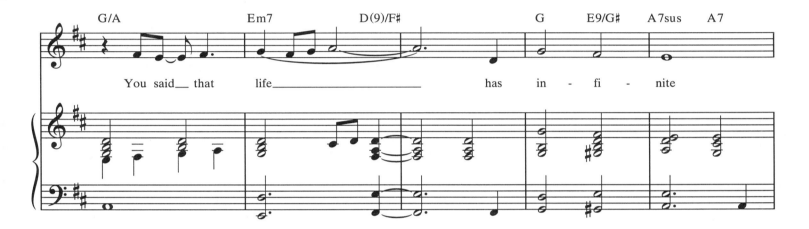

You said__ that life_____ has in-fi-nite

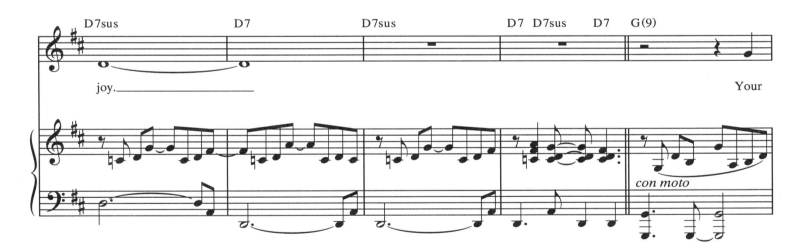

joy._____ Your

heart, your glee haunt me. Your__

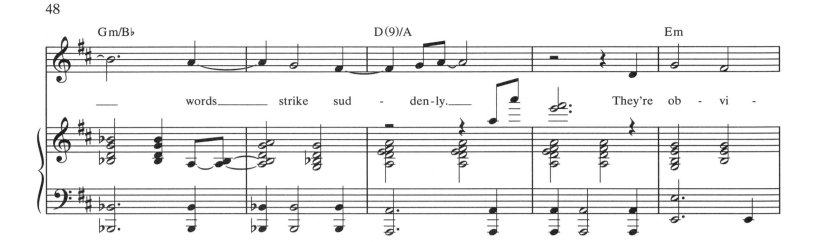

words___ strike sud-den-ly.___ They're ob-vi-

ous, but wise.___ I see the world___ through your___ eyes___ and

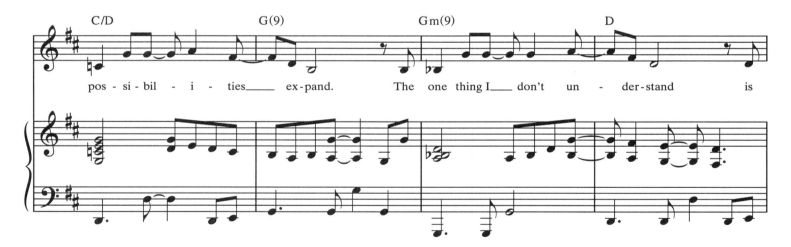

pos-si-bil-i-ties___ ex-pand. The one thing I___ don't un-der-stand is

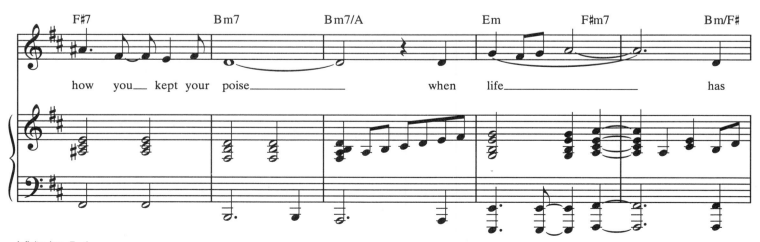

how you___ kept your poise___ when life___ has

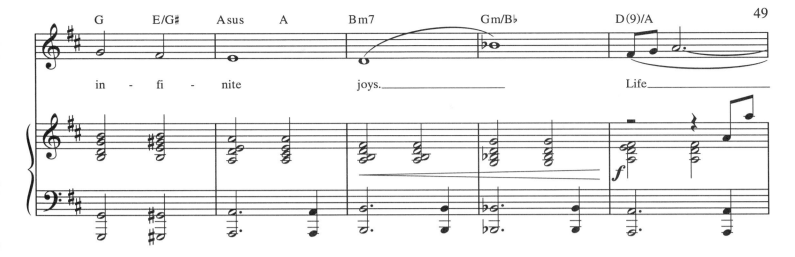

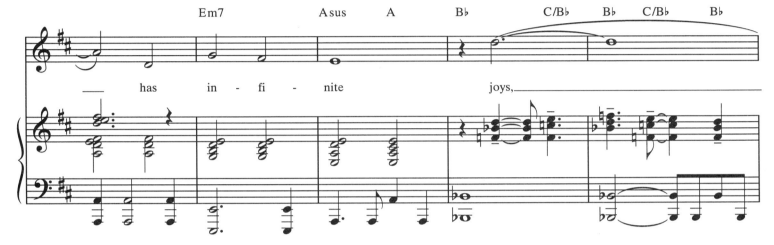

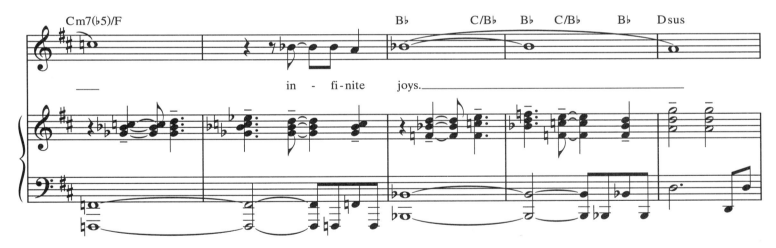

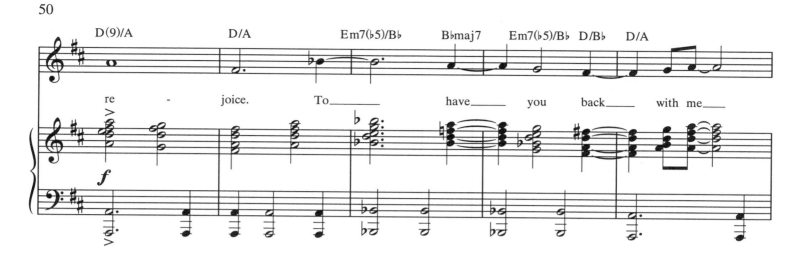

re - joice. To___ have___ you back___ with me___

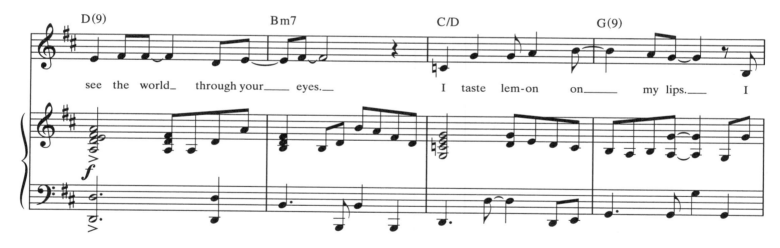

is such a fine sur - prise.___ I

see the world_ through your___ eyes.___ I taste lem-on on___ my lips.___ I

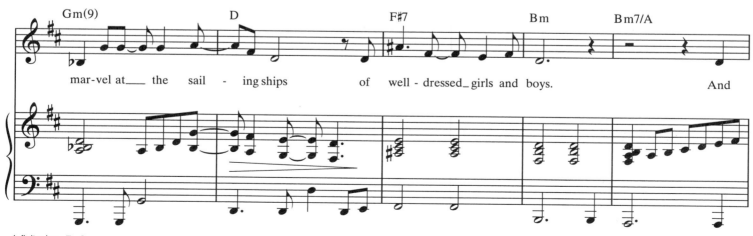

mar-vel at___ the sail - ing ships of well - dressed_ girls and boys. And

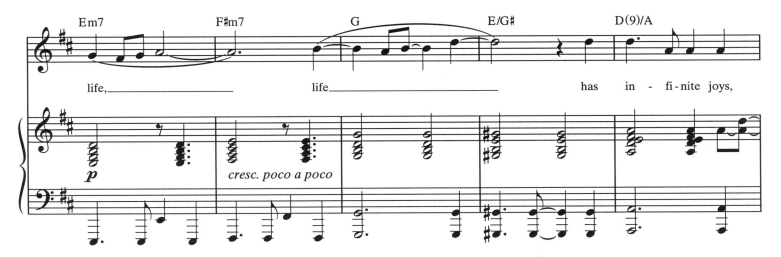

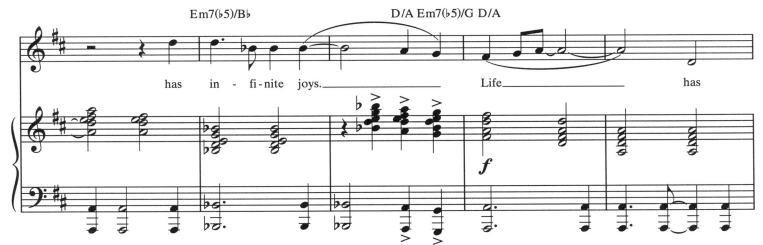

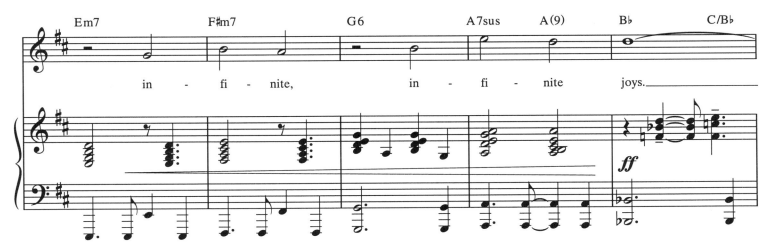

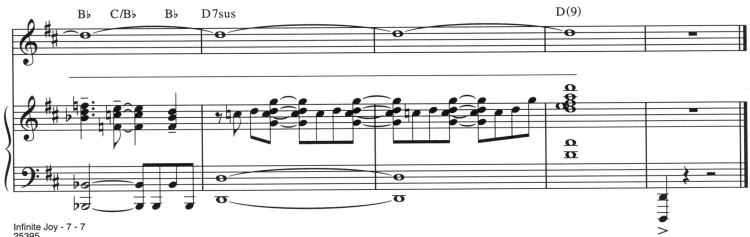

Infinite Joy - 7 - 7
25395

ANYTIME (I AM THERE)

Words and Music by
WILLIAM FINN

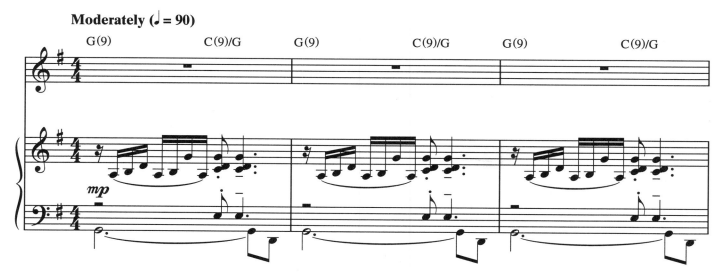

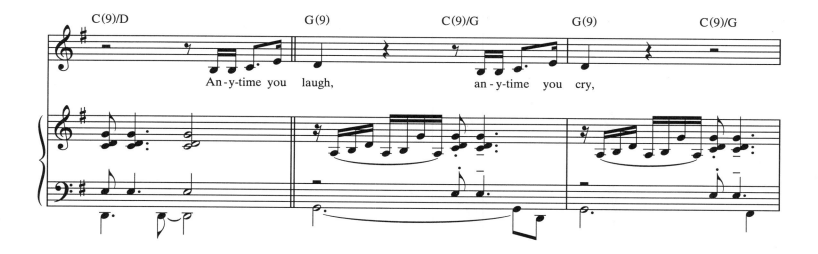

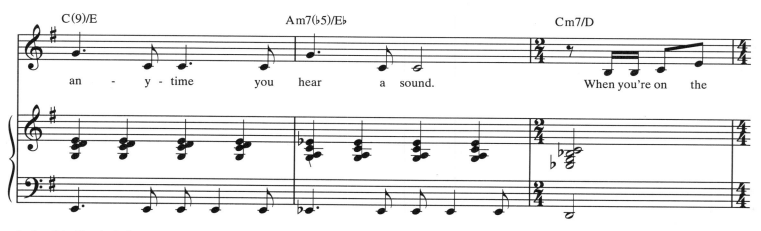

Anytime (I Am There) - 9 - 1
25395

Anytime (I Am There) - 9 - 2
25395

An-y-time.___ No, not an-y-time.___ And I am there___ each morn-

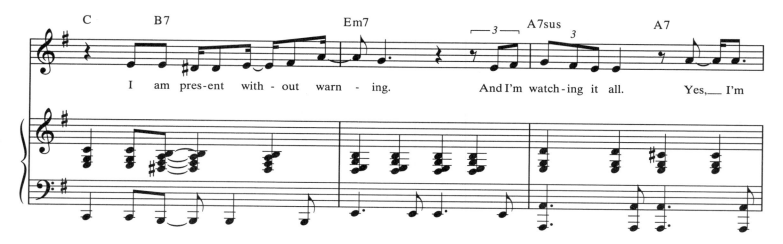

ing.___ I am there___ each___ fall.

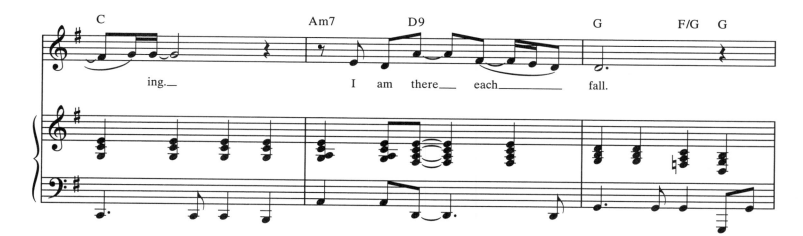

I am pres-ent with-out warn - ing. And I'm watch-ing it all. Yes,___ I'm

watch-ing it all. Oh,___ and I am there___ in mu - sic.___

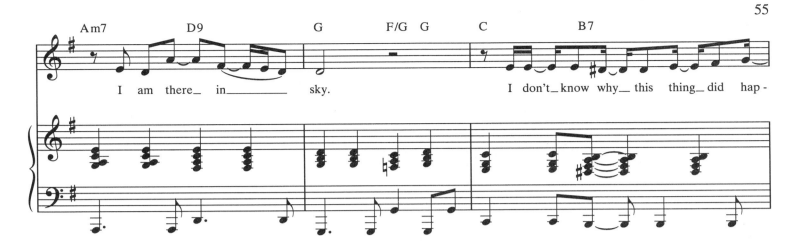

I am there in sky. I don't know why this thing did hap-

pen but this much is clear, anytime or anywhere,

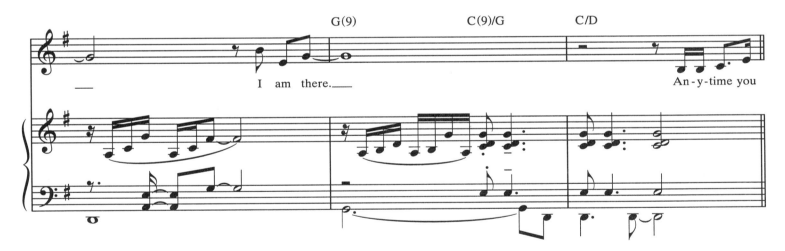

I am there. Anytime you

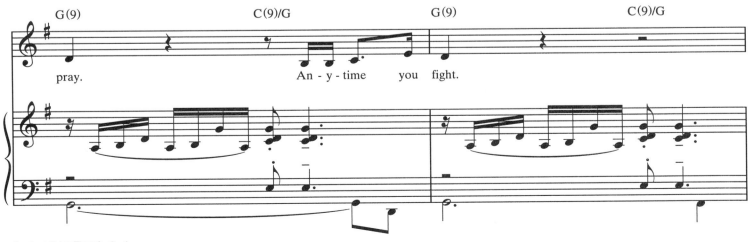

pray. Anytime you fight.

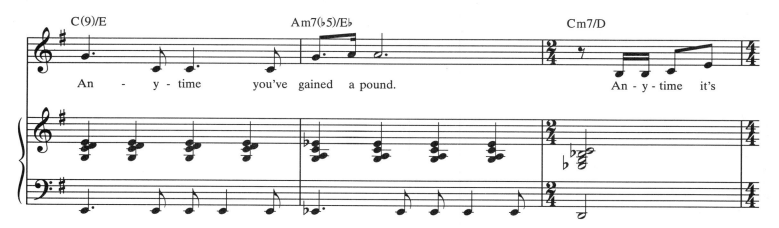

An - y - time you've gained a pound.
An - y - time it's

day. An - y - time it's___ night.___ An - y - time___ the Earth___

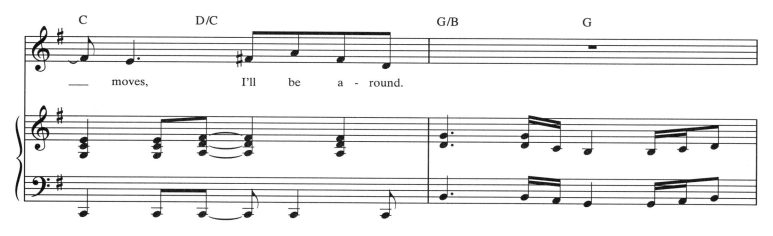

___ moves, I'll be a - round.

I'll be there in the ma - ple trees,___ I'm a sum - mer breeze___ on a per - fect eve - ning.

I'll be there when you cel - e - brate_ when the world_ seems great,_ I'll be wait-ing by___ your side.__

_ An - y - time._____ Yes! An - y - time._____ And

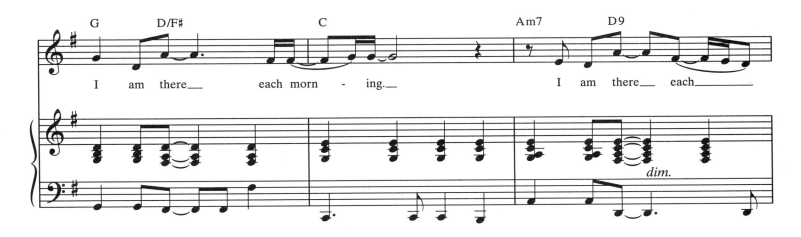

I am there___ each morn - ing.__ I am there___ each_____

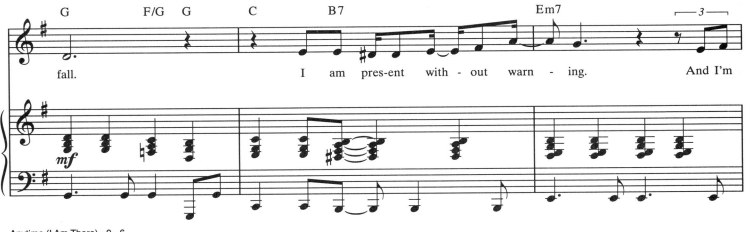

fall. I am pres-ent with-out warn - ing. And I'm

watch-ing it all. Yes,___ I'm watch-ing it all. Oh,_____ and

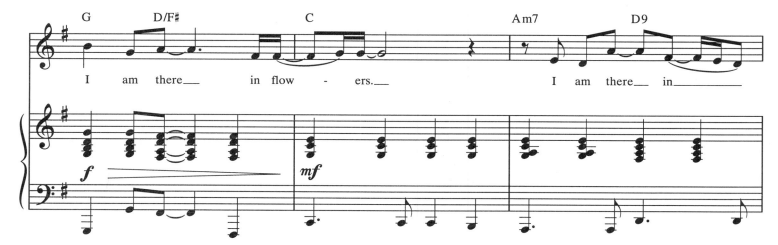

I am there___ in flow - ers.___ I am there___ in_____

snow. I don't know___ why this___ thing hap - pened but this___ much is clear,___

___ an - y - time you cry, an - y - time you

60

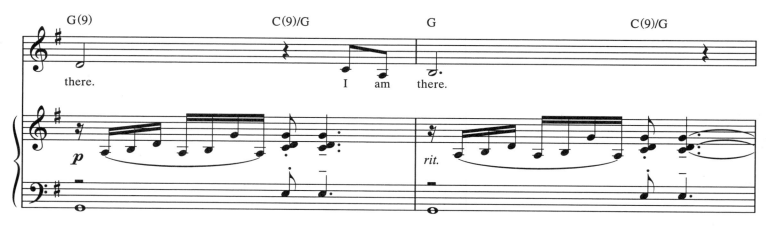

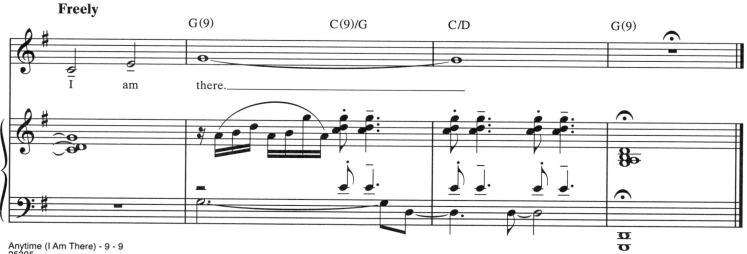

Anytime (I Am There) - 9 - 9
25395

MY DOGS

Words and Music by
WILLIAM FINN

Moderately (♩ = 84)

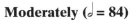

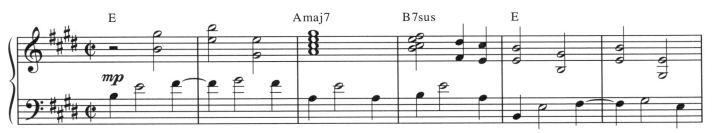

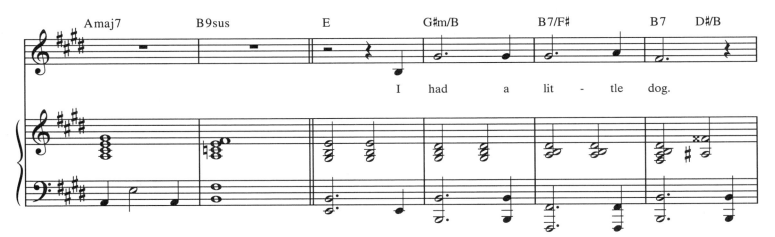

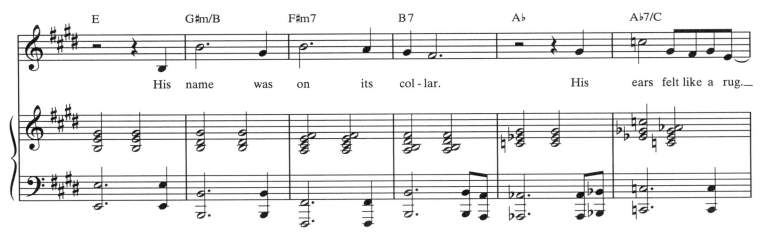

My Dogs - 9 - 1
25395

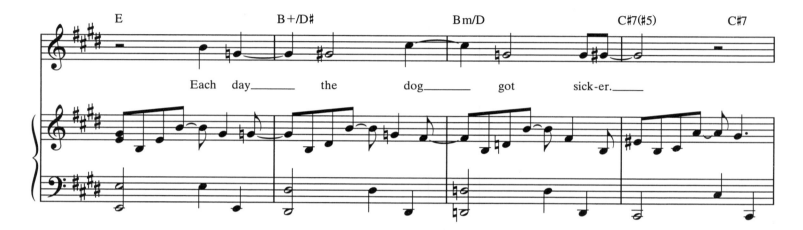

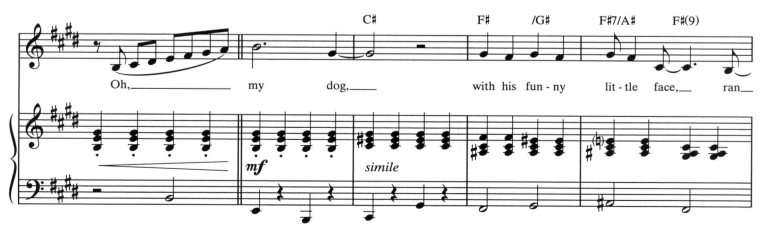

a-round this run-down place and one day, he died. My

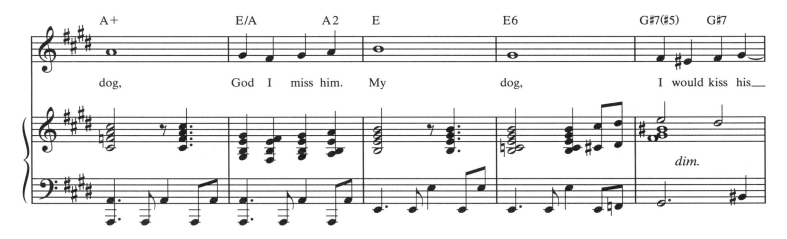

dog, God I miss him. My dog, I would kiss his

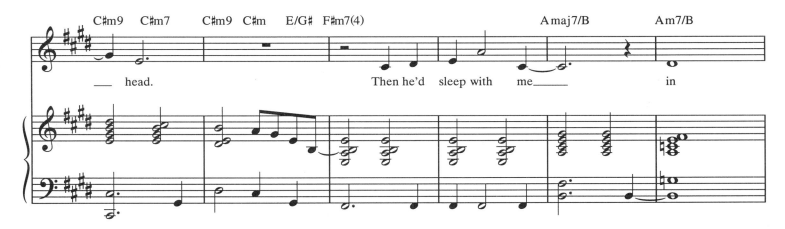

head. Then he'd sleep with me in

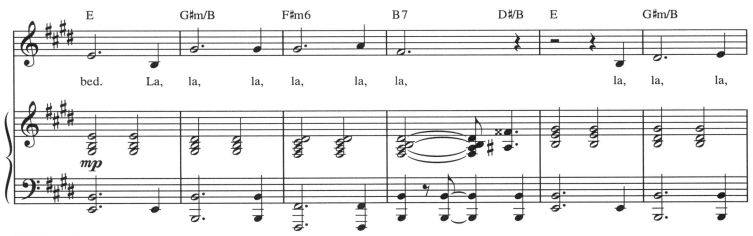

bed. La, la, la, la, la, la, la, la, la,

My Dogs - 9 - 3
25395

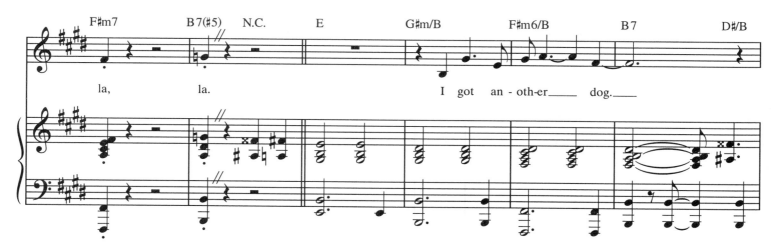

la, la. I got an-oth-er____ dog.____

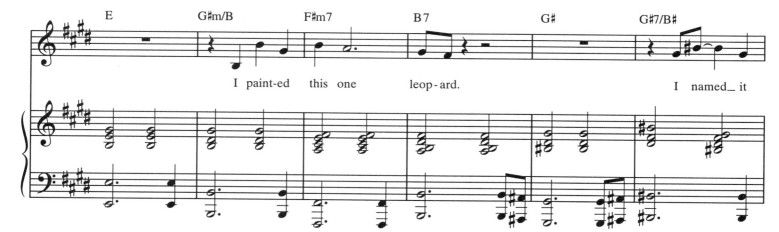

I paint-ed this one leop-ard. I named__ it

Leop-ard Spot.____ He was born a Ger - man shep - herd.____

(laughs) We'd laugh,____ the dog____ and me.____

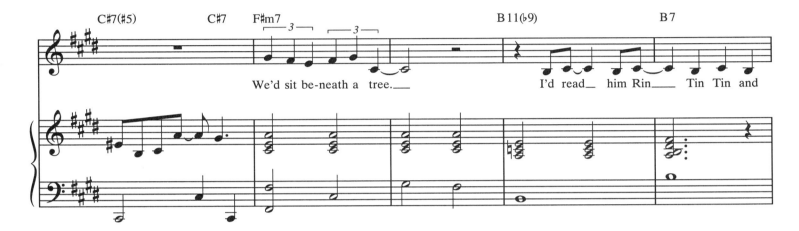

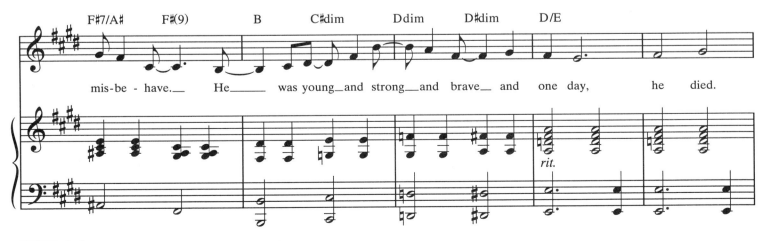

My Dogs - 9 - 5
25395

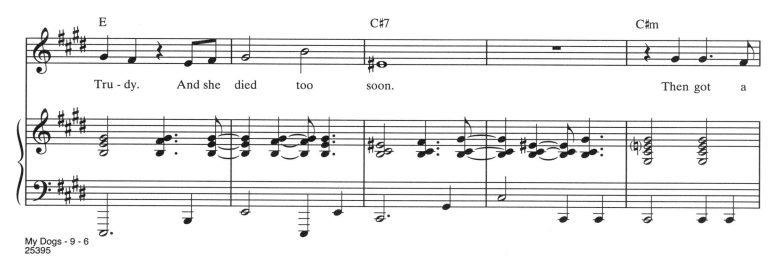

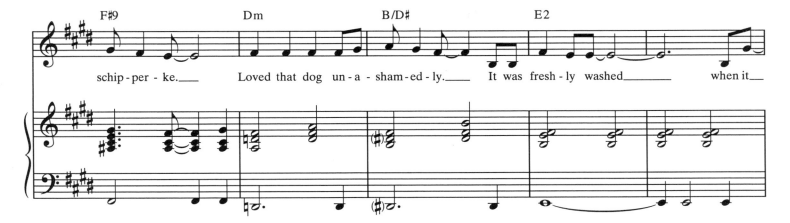

schip-per-ke.___ Loved that dog un-a-sham-ed-ly.___ It was fresh-ly washed_____ when it___

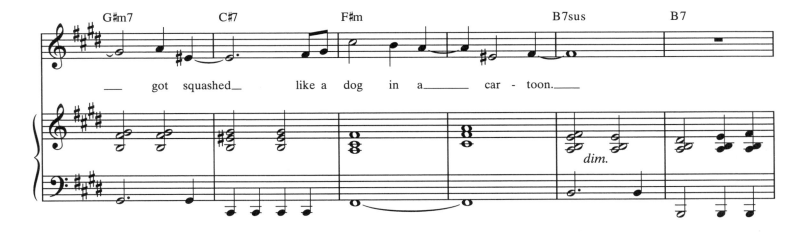

___ got squashed___ like a dog in a_____ car - toon.___

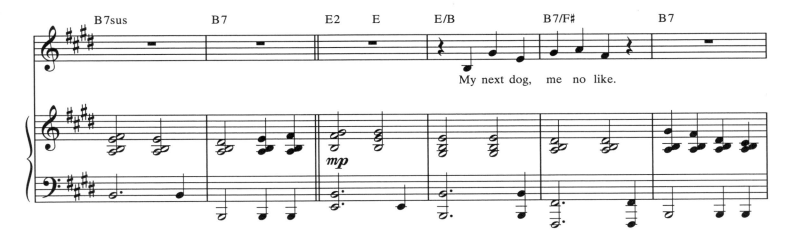

My next dog, me no like.

A Dan - die Din-mont was he. I used to toss the ca - nine

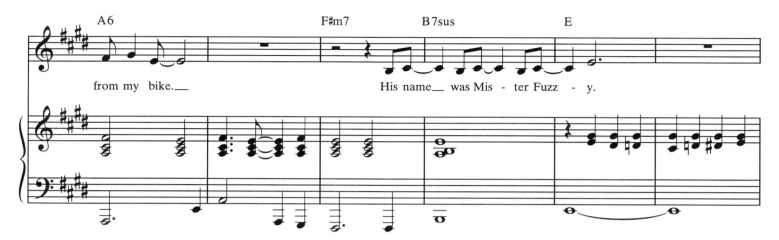

from my bike.___ His name___ was Mis - ter Fuzz - y.

I tried____ to change____ his size.____ I pushed_

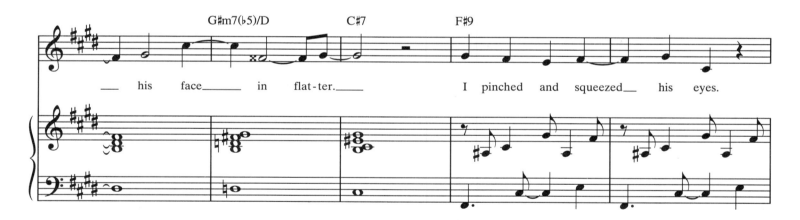

___ his face_____ in flat-ter.___ I pinched and squeezed___ his eyes.

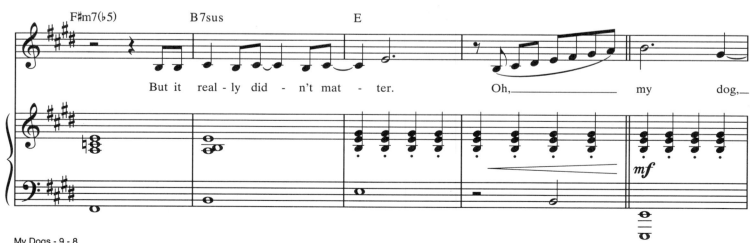

But it real-ly did - n't mat - ter. Oh,_____ my dog,_

stu-pid lit-tle Dan-die D.___ I loathed it and it___ loathed me. It lived FOR-

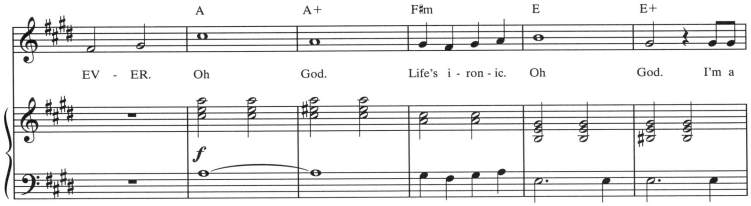

EV - ER. Oh God. Life's i - ron - ic. Oh God. I'm a

Freely

cat - a - ton - ic guy. Why's it on - ly dogs I love

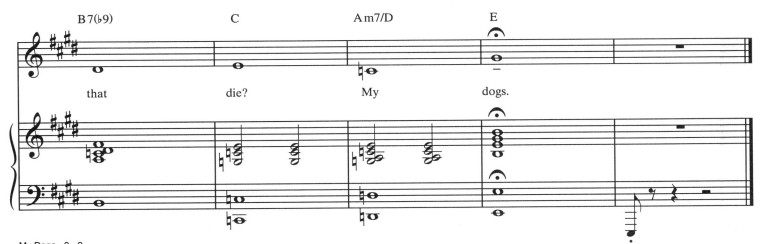

that die? My dogs.

14 DWIGHT AVE., NATICK, MASSACHUSETTS

Words and Music by
WILLIAM FINN

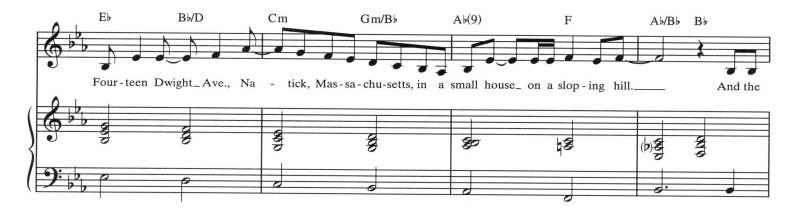

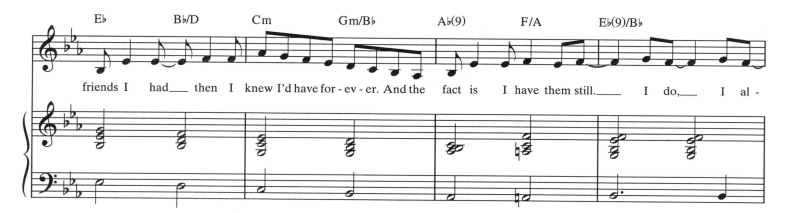

14 Dwight Ave., Natick, Massachusetts - 15 - 1
25395

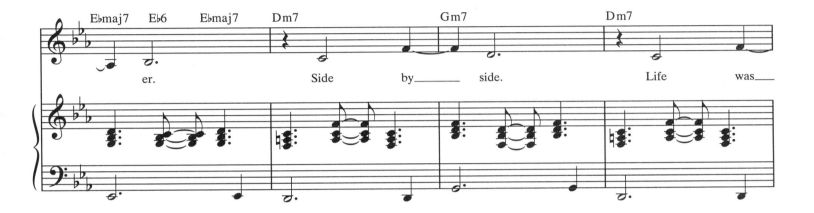

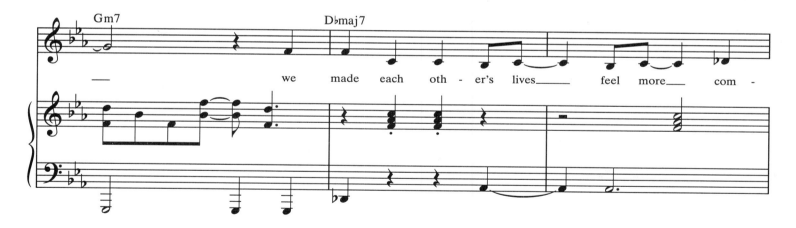

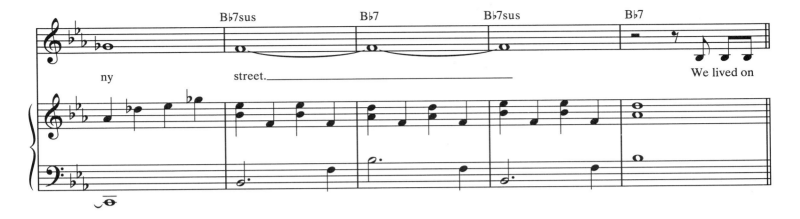

ny street._____ We lived on

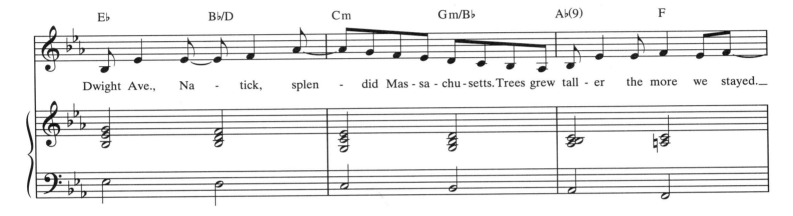

Dwight Ave., Na-tick, splen - did Mas-sa-chu-setts. Trees grew tall-er the more we stayed.__

__ As the kids grew, some hus-bands died__ in Mas-sa-chu-setts. But the wom-en were strong and un -

a - fraid.__ And rare - ly prayed.__ We were rais - ing_____ our

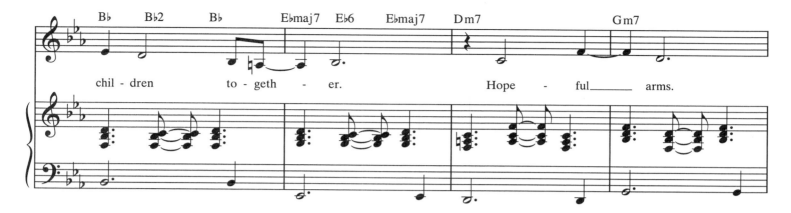

chil - dren to - geth - er. Hope - ful_____ arms.

Danc - ing_____ feet. Oh, luck - y us_____ for

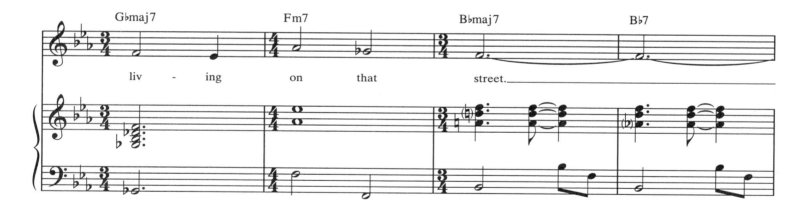

liv - ing on that street._____

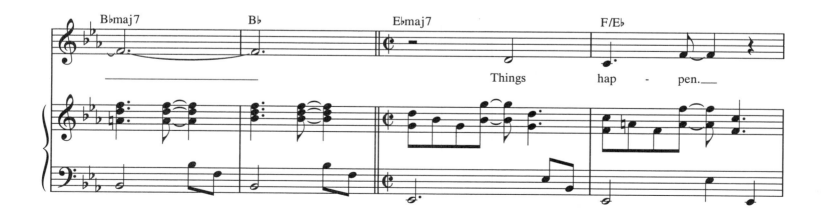

Things hap - pen._____

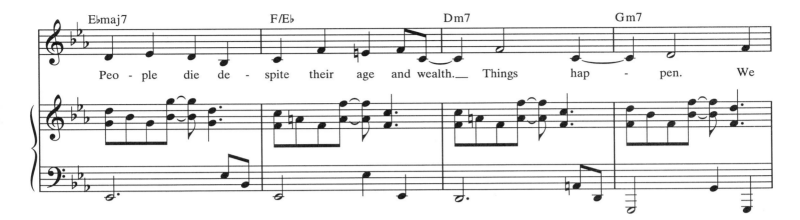

Eᵇmaj7　　F/Eᵇ　　Dm7　　Gm7

Peo - ple die de - spite their age and wealth.___ Things hap - pen. We

Dm7　　Gm7　　Dᵇmaj7

die our - selves.___ My young - est son, the sweet - est boy___ a -

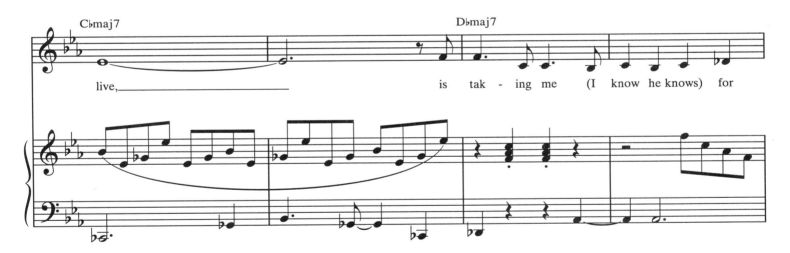

Cᵇmaj7　　Dᵇmaj7

live,_____ is tak - ing me (I know he knows) for

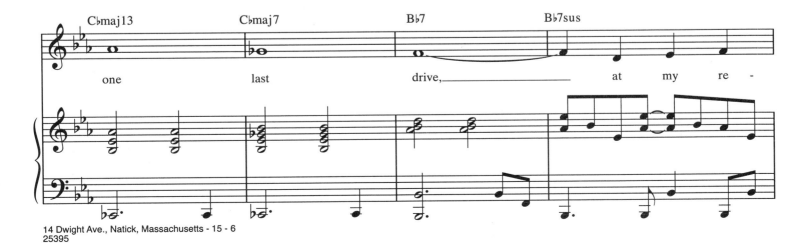

Cᵇmaj13　　Cᵇmaj7　　Bᵇ7　　Bᵇ7sus

one last drive,_____ at my re -

14 Dwight Ave., Natick, Massachusetts - 15 - 6
25395

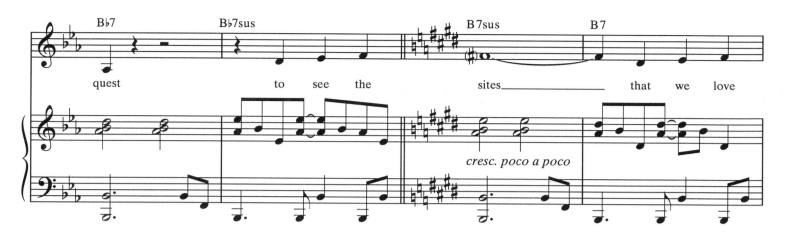

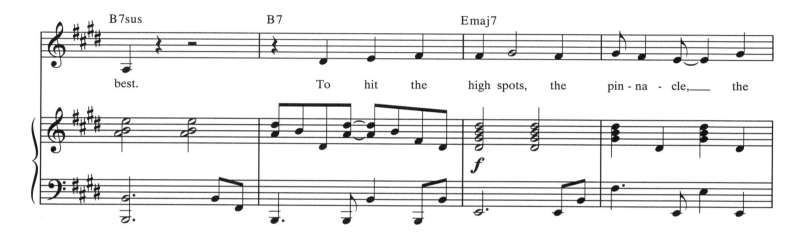

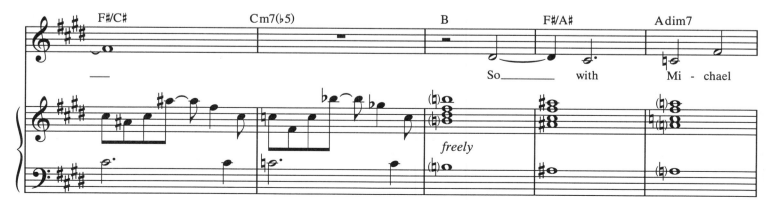

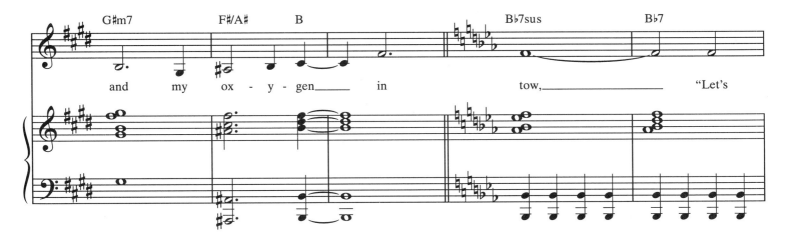

and my ox - y - gen___ in tow,_____ "Let's

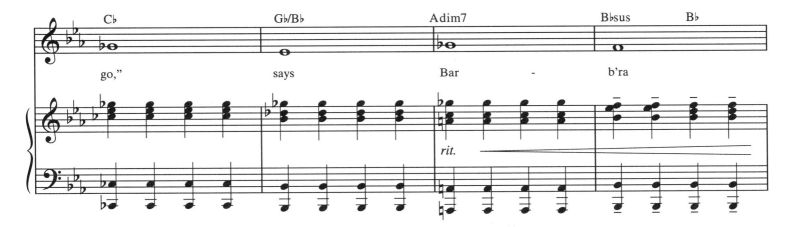

go,"   says   Bar - b'ra

Finn._____ "Let's

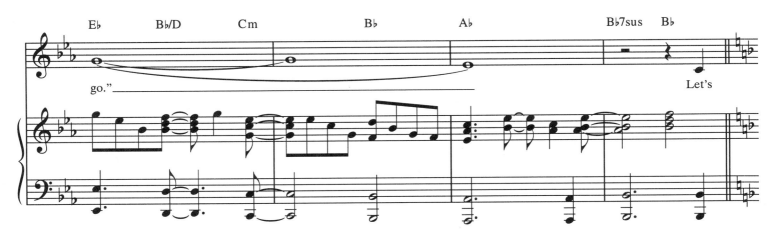

go."_____ Let's

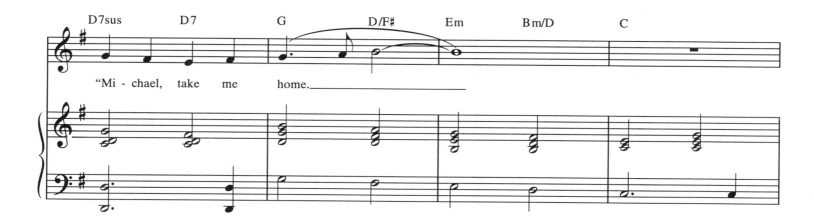

"Mi - chael, take me home._____

Mi - chael, take me home," to Four-teen Dwight_ Ave., Na -

tick Mas-sa-chu-setts, and the mem'-ries came hard as wood._____ There's Char-lotte, my dear, dear Char-

lotte, mak-ing tzim-mes for the whole dis-be-liev-ing neigh - bor-hood,_ it's so____ damn good._

moving into tempo

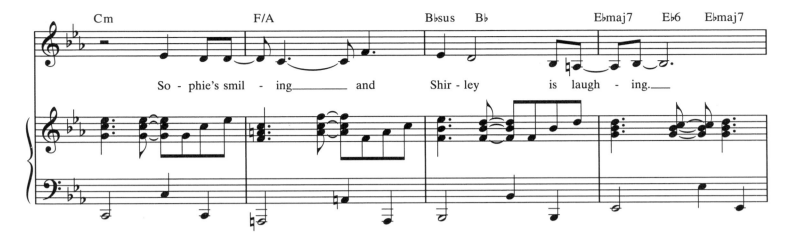

So - phie's smil - ing_____ and Shir - ley is laugh - ing._____

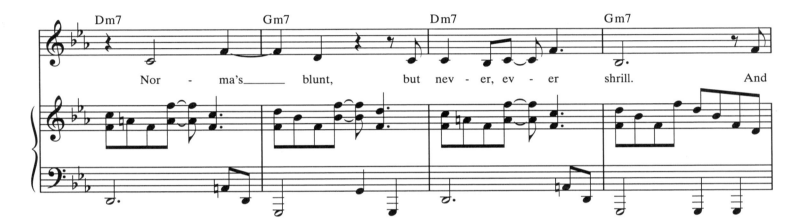

Nor - ma's_____ blunt, but nev - er, ev - er shrill. And

I'm so_____ damn luck - y to have lived here._____ It's a

crime we've so lit - tle time to kill. But

I'm blessed_____ by peo-ple who have lived here_____ and I__

__ see them_____ still._____ We lived at

Four-teen Dwight_ Ave., Na - tick, Mas-sa-chu-setts, in a small house on a slop - ing

hill.

WHEN THE EARTH STOPPED TURNING

Words and Music by
WILLIAM FINN

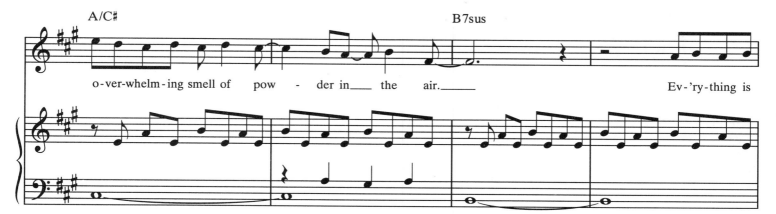

o-ver-whelm-ing smell of pow - der in___ the air.___ Ev-'ry-thing is

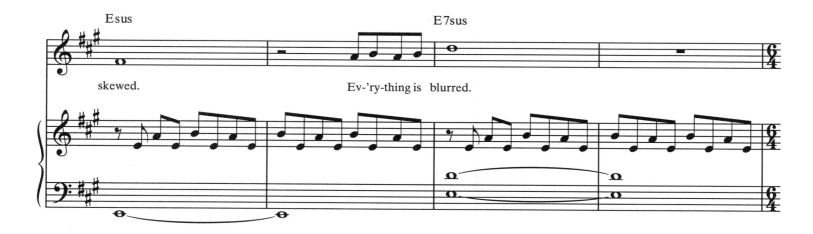

skewed. Ev-'ry-thing is blurred.

I re - mem - ber ev - 'ry word.___

I re-mem-ber how we roared,___

laughed so hard we al-most cried,_____ laughed so long, it felt the earth stopped

turn - ing._____ We were nev-er, ev - er bored and you

made us feel a-maz - ing. We were blaz-ing through our lives like com - ets in___ the sky.___

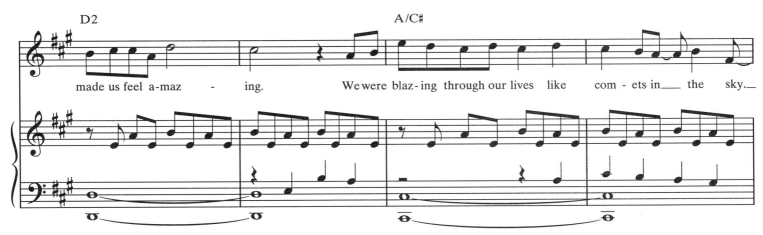

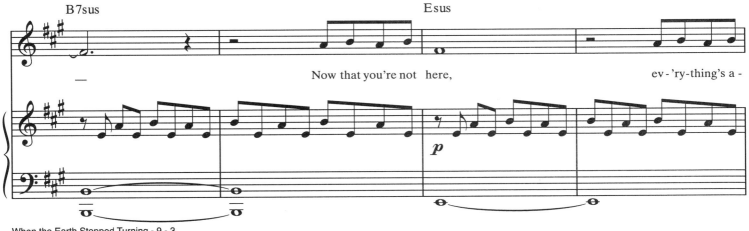

Now that you're not here, ev-'ry-thing's a-

The world is good, you said. En-joy its

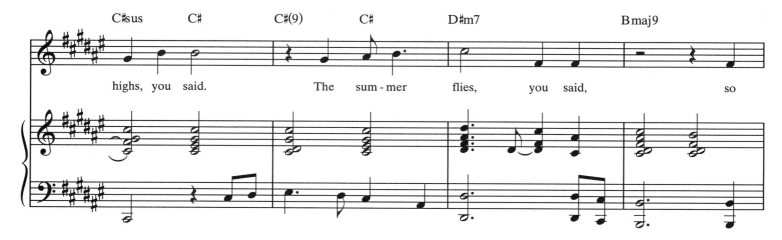

highs, you said. The sum-mer flies, you said, so

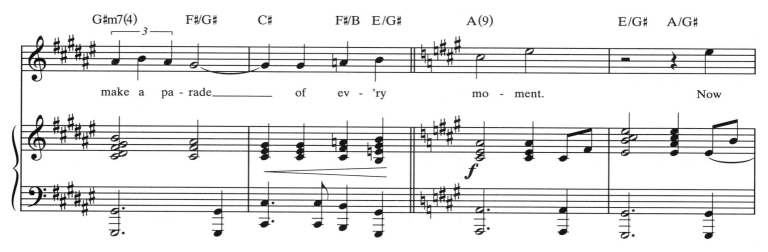

make a pa-rade_____ of ev-'ry mo-ment. Now

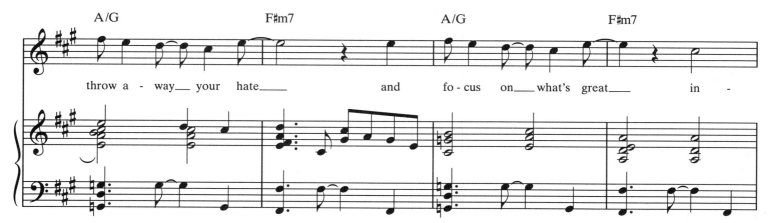

throw a-way_ your hate____ and fo-cus on___ what's great___ in-

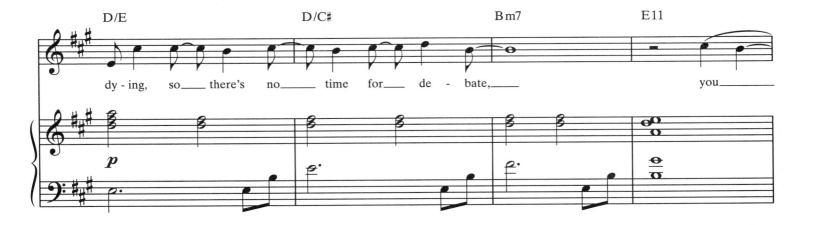

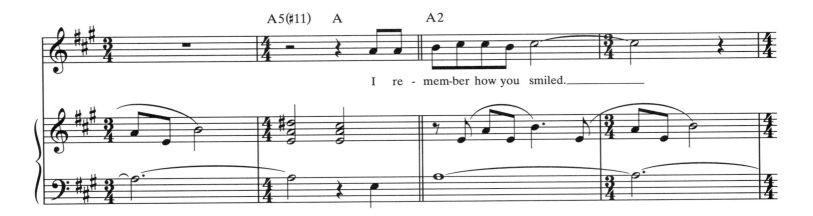

You were try-ing not to smile,_____ then you smil-ed and the earth stopped

turn - ing._____ All the im - ag - es are filed, all the

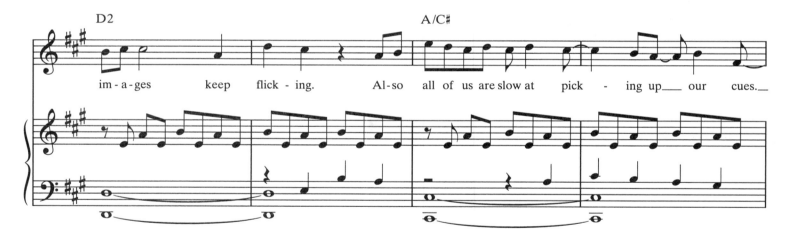

im - a - ges keep flick - ing. Al-so all of us are slow at pick - ing up___ our cues.___

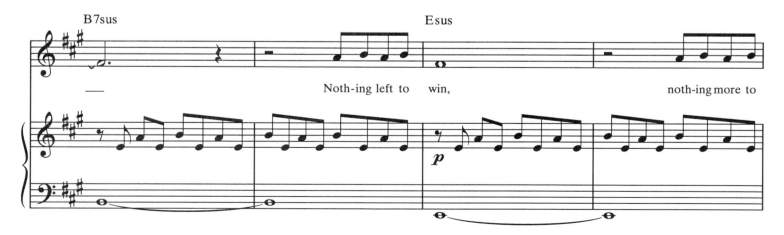

Noth-ing left to win, noth-ing more to

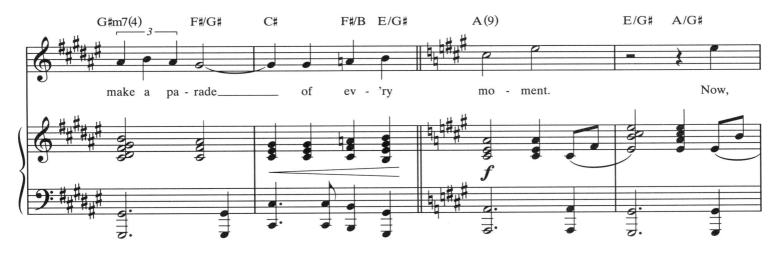

ver - y qui-et way,   I re - mem-ber how the earth___

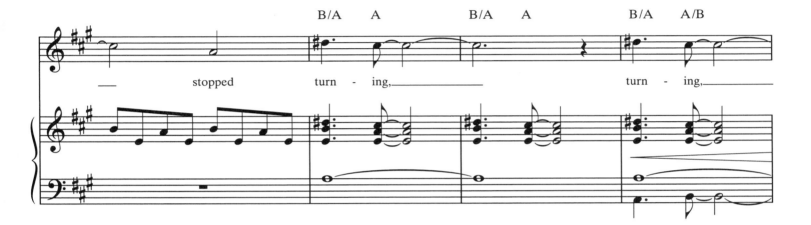

stopped   turn - ing,___   turn - ing,___

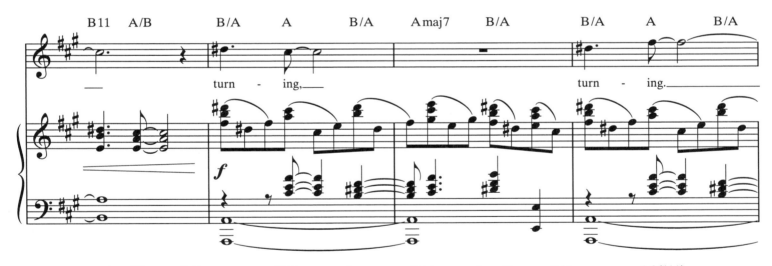

turn - ing,___   turn - ing.___

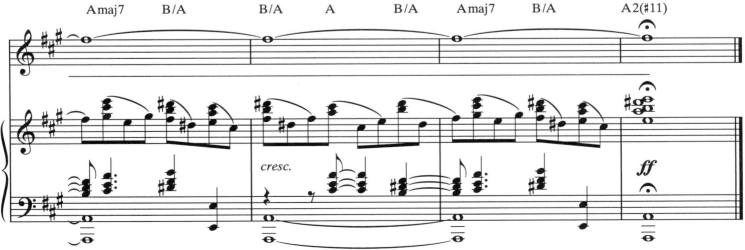

SAYING MY GOODBYES

Words and Music by
WILLIAM FINN

I would like to say___ it's been_ a priv - 'lege___ liv - ing my life___ with you.___ Who would have bet when we met things would turn out as well as they did?___

We had a sweet, re - mark - a - ble kid, the

first of an ex - pect - ed four. I'm think - ing we won't

have man - y more.____ Hey,____

_ I'm say - ing my_ good - byes.____ The

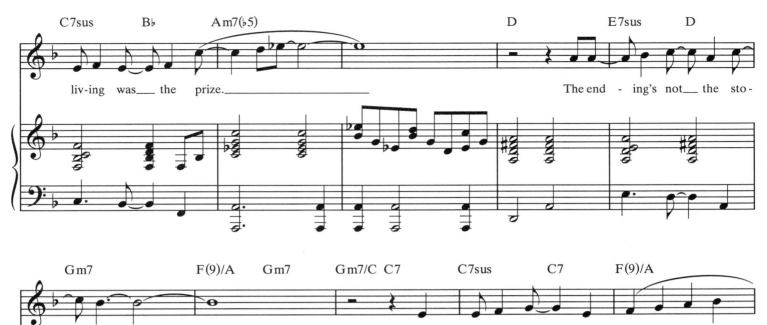

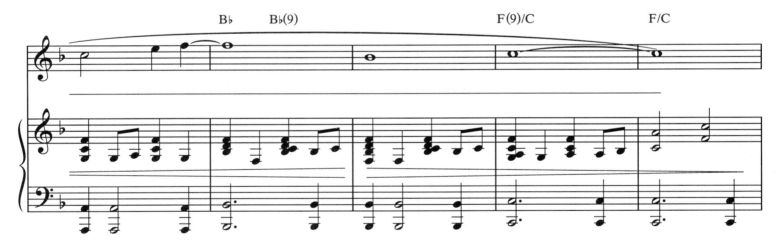

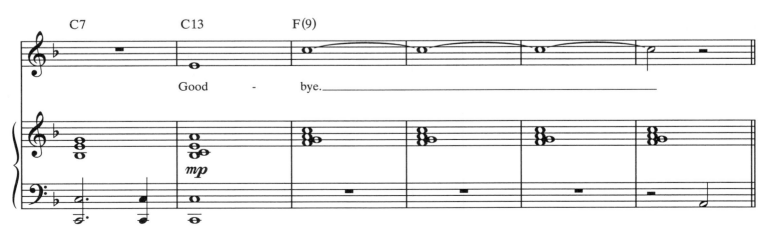

Tell the per - fect child___ I was - n't per - fect,_____ ex - cept

in lov - ing him._____ I___ ex - pect

I'm cor - rect when I say he's the salt of the earth._____

Re-mem-ber, my love, the day of his birth_____ when

I sang goof - y songs and wept? I thought that we____ had____

____ it all,____ ex - cept...____ Now,____

____ I'm say - ing my____ good - byes._____ The

liv - ing was____ the prize._____ The end - ing's not____ the sto-